I MARRIED A MINISTER

I Married
A Minister

Edited by
GOLDA ELAM BADER

ABINGDON-COKESBURY PRESS
New York ● Nashville

SET UP, PRINTED, AND BOUND BY THE
PARTHENON PRESS AT NASHVILLE, TEN-
NESSEE, UNITED STATES OF AMERICA

CONTENTS

5

INTRODUCTION

GOLDA ELAM BADER

TRAVELING HOME from Mexico City last summer, I shared my space on the train with a young American boy who with his parents was returning to the United States after a vacation in Old Mexico.

After a while this young man turned to me and said, "What do you do?"

"I am the wife of a Christian minister," I replied.

He didn't say much to this; so I continued reading my book. Soon I heard his young voice asking me, "What do you suggest that I do to entertain myself on this train?"

Closing my book, I replied, "How about talking with me? Suppose you name ten persons of the past or present that you would wish to have with you if you were shipwrecked on a desert island, and tell me why you would choose those particular people."

I was startled to hear his honest if tactless reply, "Well, I wouldn't want a preacher or his wife along. Oh, they might be all right, but they would certainly cramp my style. Why, I couldn't say what I thought, and I'll bet I couldn't even think as I pleased. And another thing—I just wouldn't want *any* women."

Over the entrance to a women's club in Bombay, India, are the words: "The world was made for women too." There is a never, ever old question as to whether or not this is a man's world. Some believe that the minds of men dominate the

7

world, and that the thinking of men has placed women in psychological straitjackets. Others would contend that this is a woman's world, and may urge us to remember that it was made for men too. I agree with Alfred Tennyson:

> The woman's cause is man's; they rise or sink
> Together, dwarf'd or godlike, bond or free.

The important thing to remember is what we, men *and* women, are doing in this world. We all live for something, and the thing a person lives for does make a difference in his thinking and acting. The size of a circle is measured from its center, and if the center of one's life is known, it is possible to judge how large is the circle of that life.

Today we all know there is need for every person's highest and best contribution in time and service. This is especially true now when we are living under world conditions that one would say cannot be, but that are. Many of us have not yet begun to apply one-tenth of our mental and spiritual force to the solution of the inescapable and pressing problems of these days. Now and then we blindly and unseeingly, while great forces are in motion, fritter away our tremendous potentialities in petty concerns of gossip and amusement. Yet, fortunately, there are countless numbers of women who refuse to be content with conditions as they are and who deliberately invest their lives in the building of a better world. Foremost among these are a group who have dedicated themselves through the men they married—the wives of ministers.

Any picture of the minister's wife must be a composite, for these women are as varied as other human beings. Hence this book, which is an endeavor to paint a partial picture of the minister's wife—her problems, her accomplishments, her possibilities—is likewise a composite. Fifteen representative wives of ministers have contributed chapters on aspects of being a minister's wife; and, for fuller perspective, two women who are not ministers' wives have presented their more objective views in the opening and closing chapters.

There is much of beauty and charm in this picture. The minister's wife is often a great personality; it takes a great woman to be the successful wife of a great man. She faces life with a high heart in spite of difficulties that might bring discouragement and defeat. With head erect and eyes alight, she makes herself a channel for the love of God. Like any wife, she is first of all a homemaker. Her greatest work is the apparently humble one of providing creature comforts, of building a haven of rest and inspiration for her husband, of sheltering and teaching the next generation. There is plenty of evidence to show how well she has succeeded in creating the Christian home. But the home is only a part of her work. She is a leader in church and community and concerns herself with matters of world-wide moment. The chapters in this book can present only a portion of her many activities and interests. Perhaps the best that can be said of her is that she is a loyal coworker with her husband in their labors to bring the Kingdom of God to earth.

One day on top of the Jungfrau, Switzerland's best-known mountain, while a storm was raging, a woman asked me: "As a minister's wife, what do you find is the greatest thing in the world to you? Is it love, or money, or power? Just what do you live for?"

These are difficult questions to answer honestly, even on a mountaintop. I tried to tell this woman that I believe the greatest thing in the world is power to live the victorious life under all conditions.

"But," she replied, "I don't think that is enough to live for. Surely a minister's wife lives for much more than victory in her own life. Sometimes, of course, life demands courage and sacrifice, and these are not too difficult to give. But one of the cries that is going up in the world is, 'Give us Life!' What are you doing about this cry?"

The minister's wife considers it a part of her own victorious life that she should hear the cries of the world and help others to hear them, giving aid in so far as she can. Often she helps by mere sympathetic listening to them; listening can be a dynamic force. Certainly, so far as her influence extends, she can be a creator of good will, and there is no greater thing to which she can give her life. For example, our American melting pot contains people of Anglo-Saxon, Irish, Scandinavian, Teutonic, Slavic, Latin, and Negro blood, to say nothing of numerous smaller groups; our citizens worship as Protestants, Roman Catholics, Jews, and other minor sects. It is the American dream, the Christian dream, that these many racial, national, and religious subgroups may blend to produce a unified, truly civilized culture. The minister's wife helps to keep that dream alive.

Here is the Good Will Creed of one minister's wife:

1. I believe in my religion and grant others the right to believe in theirs, and I respect their beliefs.

2. I believe in democracy, and that its essence is equality of opportunity for all.

3. I believe in the good life for all—good life on its several levels, material, social, emotional.

4. I believe in the worth of the individual, and I am in a conspiracy of appreciation and understanding of others.

5. I believe races are equal. Membership in my race is for me an accident; therefore I do not feel superior or inferior to people of other races.

6. I believe in freedom of speech even if it is exercised in opposition to the things to which I give my allegiance; those who disagree with me may be as good citizens or Christians as I.

7. I believe in the power of good will, and will invite into my home not only those who think as I do, but people who differ from me in religion, race, and politics; and I will respect them in these differences.

8. I believe it possible to have a world free from wars, poverty, slums, sweatshops, and hunger, with economic justice for all; and I will do what I can to have such a world.

9. I believe that I may cause personal sickness and sorrow to be bearers of blessing.

10. I believe that Christianity is a way of acting.

The minister's wife believes that today the measure of our lives is to be found not in any differences of culture, or of social position, or of wealth. She knows that the measure of a life is rather to be found in what passionately one wants for oneself and others, and what one is willing to do in attainment. In the heart of this woman the clamorous wants of people arise to consciousness and expression. She believes that a new world waits on the dominant hunger of men for righteousness, peace, and brotherhood; and she has dedicated her handful of days to proclaiming the Kingdom of God on earth. She believes that there will come a day when the things that ought to be true shall be made true, and when all of us can have a part in bringing that day in, even if scanning the horizon for signs of peace and good will is sometimes a disheartening experience. There may seem little in the contemporary scene to portend the Kingdom of God on earth, but none of us can afford merely to keep our good will in cold storage for a better time. Ministers' wives take action and offer leadership in all human struggles for betterment.

I

PORTRAIT OF A MINISTER'S WIFE

BESS WHITE COCHRAN

THE MOST arresting feature of my mother's appearance is her eyes. As a young woman she was tall and slender—willowy, they called it then—and was considered handsome. Her thick hair still falls in soft, natural waves from her high forehead, and she wears it yet fastened in a loose knot at her neck. Her short nose turns up impertinently over her wide, laughing mouth, but her eyes contradict the impression of a careless appraisal of the passing scene. They are of that peculiar green that suggests unfathomable depths, and they move quickly, missing nothing.

While I was still a little girl I became aware of the curious fact that my mother could detect at one glance if I had told a lie or had not washed behind the ears. Later I saw her many times bare a man's soul with a single look, evoking the sanctity of the church in the operation. Few people feel comfortable when my mother looks intently at them, although she actually sees more with her heart than with her eyes. She claims a sense of divine discernment, and her family has often seen the claim justified. She admits, however, that the gift has a practical basis, the result of a canny observation of the queer thing called human nature, plus excellent eyesight, two serviceable faculties in any minister's wife.

It was a September day at high noon when my mother laid her hand in that of my father and softly said, "I do." She was

13

barely eighteen years old. They stood before garlands of autumn branches on the porch of the hilltop farmhouse where she was born, and looked across the Ohio hills. Indian summer had already spread its purple veil, and the scent of burning wood hung pungent in the air.

As soon as the brief ceremony was over, Father and Mother ran from the confusion of relatives and climbed into a handsome surrey, hired by the young preacher bridegroom for the occasion. There was a waving of hands and a medley of farewells as the happy couple drove down the country lane that led to the dusty turnpike. At the bend of the road they paused and looked fleetingly back, and then faced about for the drive that was to lead them through fifty years together in the ministry.

Thus at eighteen my mother stepped from the simple life of a fun-loving country girl into the whirlpool of divine service tempered by human frailties that is known as a church pastorate. The recovery of poise and patience, the growth of dignity and diplomacy, the development of a new splendor and spirit is the story of her life.

The church to which my father took his bride was in central Kentucky, a fashionable congregation of bluegrass aristocrats. No better and no worse than the average, the church members reserved their religion for Sunday and cavorted in the lush fields of the world the rest of the time. To Mother, consumed with the idealism of budding young womanhood consecrated now to high endeavor, it was a strange concept of the Christian life. It was the first bugle call to ride forth on her shining white charger of duty. Barely had the ice cream melted on the lace-draped reception tables when the minister's young bride took up the reins. Nothing less is suggested by the historic

14

ride, now a family legend, which she took roughshod over the derelictions of the card-playing, dancing church members. Fearless denunciation of such activities marked her route as she arose in prayer meeting, in the Ladies' Aid Society, and in lesser groups to speak her mind. From all accounts it was the equivalent of a modern blitz. Father, slightly more experienced in the ministry, hesitated, warned by some realistic instinct, and then loyally joined her.

As soon as the church members recovered their breath and their equilibrium, a battle royal ensued. To the parishioners, my mother's was a brand of Christianity they had not bargained for; their private lives were not within the province of the church. To the minister's crusading young wife, nothing less than the whole of life belonged to the church. The battle raged in board meetings, over the dinner tables, on the street, through the pews, and out from the pulpit. It even hit the pages of the town's bi-weekly newspaper.

Hearing the story in later years, I have often regretted that it could not have been fought to a finish and thus have furnished a badly needed test case in ecclesiastical boundary disputes. But kindly Providence, aided and abetted no doubt by human agencies, intervened; and a call hurriedly came to the young ministers from a church in another part of the state. They accepted, upon advice of all concerned, and with heads bloody but unbowed turned to other fields. Their initiation into the splendor of spiritual service was complete. For my mother, no longer was the ministry an idyllic ritual; from then on her work smelled of blood and sweat; and, although it was tempered, as the years advanced, by sweet charity and humor, it gained in power and glory.

Ironically enough, as the day of parting drew near, the hearts of some of the more belligerent members softened, and many love offerings found their way to the parsonage door. On the evening before departure, the whole church turned out and stormed the house, presenting the young couple with enduring gifts—to father a watch, and to Mother a rope of gold beads. The gifts were accepted as the peace offerings they were, and were worn for years in humility and in pride.

From Kentucky, Father's ministry led him to the West, then young and lusty with life. Included in the family group that made the long trip across the continent with Father and Mother were my sister and I, both of us toddling babies, and my father's two younger bachelor brothers, one a lawyer and the other a doctor, both seeking fame and fortune in the new country. For us all Mother was the central pivot, guiding, advising, encouraging, tirelessly laboring. How we all managed to squeeze into the small third-floor flat Father rented in San Francisco is a miracle, but how we all lived there together for three years in peace and harmony is testimony to Mother's managerial capacity and her transcending, contagious sense of humor.

For eight years—developing and determining years, fruitful years—my parents labored in San Francisco, caught in the current of world forces, touching hands with the Orient, building a great church out of the youth and vigor of that glamorous city by the Golden Gate. Then back to the Midwest for a decade of turmoil and triumph, of bitter hardship and compensating joy, and finally to his native state of Tennessee, Father's pastorates took him. By his side through it all strode his wife, always alert and eager, inspired and inspiring. Her children now numbered five, all girls, and her hands and heart were full to overflowing.

16

To this day the odor of homemade bread sharply recalls my mother. During the period when her children were growing up, covering a span of over eighteen years, Mother made regularly twenty-one loaves of bread a week; and on Wednesdays and Sundays she made hot biscuits. She did all the cooking and laundry, and all of the housecleaning with the exception of the work she could get out of her day-dreaming daughters. Such physical labor is not conducive to the spiritual meditation in which my mother delighted, and which she no doubt needed; but never did I hear her complain. She was strong and able, and considered it her end of the bargain. And gradually her end increased until, by tacit understanding, her share of the task of ministering to a church took in the oversight if not the active management of most of the church's sweeping program.

This was not due to any shifting of the burden by Father, but was the result of Mother's prudent foresight. As her homemaking duties increased, she recognized the threat of absorption in such mechanics and determined to hold paramount her role of high priestess. She refused to be turned from her high calling by the connivance of prosaic circumstance.

I think she caught the mystery and magic of her work more than any of us realized at the time. In season and out, the church and its ongoing was uppermost in her mind. She loved the church with all her heart and proved it with both hands, although her concern for some individuals in it was rooted in a sense of responsibility rather than love. Her religion was one of confidence and joy, but with piety she held no truck. Yet her fervor helped Father tremendously to maintain his faith and hope in the face of discouragement. Mother's life had many anchors. In any storm she could let one down, assured it would hold steady; and our darkest moments were

17

radiant with the light of her belief. "I know whom I have believed," was and is the cornerstone of her life.

It was in San Francisco that Mother first caught the vision of the missionary task which has burned with an unquenchable flame in her heart ever since. Missionaries going to and coming from the Orient were our constant guests, stretching our horizons and our hearts. As a result Mother became the major-domo of the missionary program in every church we subsequently served. She was not always the president of the women's missionary society, but most of the time it took on the stamp of her powerful personality. She took a personal pride in the size of the missionary offering, and felt a personal responsibility for it. Never during Father's various pastorates was any church we served anything less than a "Living-Link Church." Mother saw to it that the congregation not only supported one or more missionaries on the field, but did it joyfully. I have known her to talk down building fund committees and outflank new carpet committees in reaching that goal, but it was always reached.

At one time Father and Mother were approached by one of our missionary boards as possible candidates for service on the foreign field. They weighed the matter long and prayerfully. Their lives were dedicated to sacrificial service, and at that time it seemed that in no place was such service so sorely needed as on the foreign field. Their decision to remain in the homeland was due to several diverse factors, but an innocent remark by a board secretary acridly flavored their reaction. The genial secretary, talking with them about the proposed task, said by way of further inducement, "Actually, Brother and Sister White, foreign missionary service is not so hard; it has many advantages." Father was a bit tardy to recognize any indictment in the remark, but Mother recoiled instantly. To this day she resents it as a slander on the missionary life.

Mother is of Scottish descent and is highly endowed with the traditional Scotch tenacity. Her contempt is quick to flare at a suggestion that the road be made easier for any mortal, an attitude which her children for a long time failed to appreciate. Not only does the way of the cross lead home for Mother, but *only* the way of the cross goes in that direction. She is suspicious of any short cut to anything.

Mother would tackle any situation that needed attention, large or small. Her only known fear in life was of burglars; when her children were small she was frankly nervous when Father was away at night. At such times it was her habit to pull all the beds into one room, and lock the door. To this day not one of her children will sleep with the bedroom door open, and generally we want it locked. On these occasions Mother's weapon was characteristic of her ingenuity. We never had a gun in the house, and knives were too treacherous to handle around small children. But Mother believed in preparedness; and as we all trudged at bedtime into the one room and clamored into bed, Mother unfailingly would put down beside her bed for ready use her one weapon, a box of red pepper. No burglar ever appeared, somewhat to Father's amusement and disappointment, for he often said he wanted to see what Mother would do with her box of pepper. That she would have used it unhesitatingly to the complete rout of the burglar we had not the slightest doubt.

But if Mother lacked a little in "burglar bravery" she more than compensated for it in moral courage. She was not dogmatic, and actually had few convictions, but those few were

19

not elastic. In view of this her tolerance of human weakness was surprising. Somewhere along the way she had grasped the fact that much which passes for sin is blind frustration, and "understanding much, she condemned little." Yet when a matter of principle was involved, she would cross swords with any member of the church, regardless of his prominence or pledge-paying abilities. She was forthright; no minor keys vibrated through her personality. Although she did not scorn tact and was not above using diplomacy, if these failed she unhesitatingly, and sometimes with relish, struck straight from the shoulder. I have often suspected that in Mother's innermost heart, peace and serenity are not her idea of heaven.

Mother's tendency to undertake any task sometimes sent her skidding into the vicinity of impending catastrophe. Once she was asked to give a talk before the leading woman's club of the city on the subject "Why Our Troops are in Guatemala."

Now Mother was not a student of international relations, and her interest in America's foreign policy at that time was bounded by its effect on our mission fields. But she accepted the subject assigned without a moment's hesitation. As the time drew near for the scheduled speech, Father began getting nervous. He called to her attention several articles on the topic in current magazines, and even brought a couple of relevant books home from the library. If Mother ever read them we never caught her at it. On the day of the speech she dressed with her usual care. She was drawing on her gloves when Father appeared at the door, a little breathless. He had hurried home from a funeral, frankly apprehensive now for the success of her talk, knowing all too well her imperturbable assurance. "Mother, are you *sure* you've got your speech ready? Where—where is Guatemala? Tell me just that."

Mother gave him one look, scalding his loyal heart, and sailed blithely on her way. Alas, Father's fears were all too well founded. The talk, we heard later, was a great success. It was received with acclaim. But it was not on Guatemala. It was on the state of missionary work in India. How the daring young woman ever made the leap from the subject assigned to her to the one she spoke on, we never learned; but she managed it somehow to the satisfaction of the program committee, for they asked her back the next year, this time to speak on any subject she chose.

Mother was never one who considered poverty a blessing or a necessary attribute of the ministry. She considered the laborer worthy of his hire in the legal tender of this world as well as of the next, and impressed her views on our various official boards in ways subtle but effective. She believed in dressing herself and her family well; and although her hats were often bought in the bargain basements, she always managed to get them on at a smart angle—not too smart, but smart. She realized, for one thing, that many women who sat in the pews judged the church by the tilt of her hat.

There is something exquisitely symbolic in a habit Mother acquired of wearing her best dress, a blue chiffon, under an old one while at work about the house. She always had a navy blue chiffon. I have no idea how it was made, and it surely must have varied with the changing styles, but Mother's blue chiffon was a part of her. It was practical, inconspicuous, and becoming; and it could be worn anywhere.

In many of the parsonages we occupied there was no back stairway. If Mother was in the kitchen and a wedding couple or other callers came, there was no access to her clothes closet or dressing room without going through the front of the house.

21

Mother had been caught once in her shabbiest house dress by a couple needing a witness at their marriage; and, in spite of her denial, there is an understandable streak of human pride in the composition of her soul. She insists it is a reflection on the church to appear in shoddy clothes; but nevertheless she enjoyed, and still enjoys, a normal feminine desire to appear well dressed.

Within the twinkling of an eye, or the tinkle of the doorbell, Mother would let fall her house dress about her feet and stand forth dressed for any visitor, tucking in loose strands of her hair and running a hand over her clear, smooth face as she walked unabashed into the living room. Most visitors accepted her appearance as a matter of course; she was simply a gracious woman, always attired in simple good taste. But some of the less resourceful women in the church wondered how she did it, and several times she suspected them of deliberately trying to catch her in a disheveled state. They never did. And they never found out how she managed.

Mother's resourcefulness amazed every church we served and put to shame more than one ambling servant in the vineyard. She could plan a missionary program while doing the family laundry, and many times we children were coached for our part in the Children's Day exercises while she had us drying the dishes. One night while she was bathing the current baby she called to Father to bring her, as he heard it, more soap. Sticking his head in the bathroom door as he handed her a bar, he discovered she had suggested he preach the next Sunday a sermon on "Hope." Her formal training in economics was limited to the practice of withholding from the milkman to pay the gas bill, until the process had to be reversed; but she could plan to a penny the church budget, and make it balance.

22

Her oversight of the church included not only its major undertakings but many details which commonly are outside the concern of even the most conscientious minister's wife. And rarely was her activity resented, a tribute both to her and to her fellow workers. One Sunday morning Mother hustled us all off to Sunday school particularly early. Our family always went in a body in the family automobile; and we children disliked getting there very much in advance of the opening time, as it generally meant some task to be performed, such as folding the bulletins or distributing the songbooks. We knew on this morning that something was in store for us, but not until we arrived at the church and Mother had herded us all into the main auditorium did we discover the reason. Mother ran her hand over a pew and it came away covered with a good streak of gray dust. Without a word she tossed each of us a cloth she had brought in anticipation of the worst, and for twenty minutes the preacher's family, including the preacher, dusted the church pews. The janitor stuck his head in the door only once. The next day he told Father apologetically, "Missus White jest wears me out, Doctor White, jest watchin' her."

Mother was wiser than we realized. She never held on to the office of president of the Ladies' Aid or the missionary society or to any position of prominence too long. She would take her turn along with the rest, but she considered part of her job was to help her husband develop the latent leadership that was all too content to warm the church pews or coach from the side lines. Similarly, although she was blessed with a fine alto voice and often sang in the church choir, she never allowed any director or music committee to make her a soloist. Her voice was pleasing, and sounded to us like an angel's, but she knew that its too frequent use in the choir loft could cause disquieting reverberations in the pews.

I never saw my mother at church suppers peeling potatoes when she should have been sitting beside her husband with the guest speaker. She didn't mind peeling potatoes, and even onions, and did her share of it; but as the wife of the minister she knew that something more was expected of her than the ability to work tirelessly in the kitchen.

With all her activities in the church, Mother never neglected her children or her home. We were not coddled, but neither were we forlorn. As our life in the parsonage recedes in time, we are beginning to suspect that even in this Mother was prompted, in part at least, by her consuming concern for the church. She realized that soiled dishes left in the sink or beds left unmade because she had to rush off to a meeting at the church might be resented by her children and affect their attitude toward the church in later years. On the other hand, Mother tried honestly to divorce herself from every other relationship when dealing with her children. When we first brought home to her the problems of card playing and dancing and all the other bewildering allurements of the world, she considered us not only as children-of-the-minister-who-must-set-an-example, but as individuals who must learn to distinguish for ourselves on a fundamental basis the difference between right and wrong. She gave us the best of her guidance; she shared with us out of the richness of her experience; she directed our hearts and our eyes and our feet toward the path that she thought led straightest to the abundant life—and then she let us walk in it alone.

As her children grew older and her household responsibilities lightened, Mother assumed more and more an active part in national church work. The local church was still her first concern, and she had at her fingers' ends its program and its problems, and generally their solutions; but the larger program of the church increasingly called to her. In the course of time she was appointed to membership on every major board in our communion, and served with distinction. She worked with young people's groups, organizing and guiding through its difficult formative years the first young people's summer conference of our church in Tennessee; she interested herself in temperance and was a solicited speaker in behalf of that movement. She was in equal demand for service on carpet committees and on necrology committees. No avenue of Christian service has she left untrod since she drove down the country lane that September day into the maelstrom of the ministry.

All ministers' wives have a tremendously delicate job. Few of them probably choose such a calling deliberately. They fall in love with a dreaming youth—and there they are. But all who bear this kinship with the ministry are confronted with a peculiar opportunity. The world looks at them a little askance, and yet a little hopefully. Out of a woman's heart that beats in tune with that of a servant ordained by the Lord there should come some hint of the answer to the mystery of life. My mother, I believe, discerned this, and she answered in a thousand little ways—not only in words, but in homely acts and honest attitudes that spoke of courage, understanding, vision, and a sublime faith. For some ministers' wives these are acquired characteristics, but for my mother they were bred in the bone. That was her glory.

II

HER CHURCH

PRISCILLA WAHL STAMM

"WELL, Mary, I never thought you would marry a minister," was an older friend's greeting the day after Mary's engagement had been announced.

"Neither did I," said Mary, "but I am marrying the man I love and not his profession."

The friend smilingly expressed her good wishes for Mary's wedded happiness, knowing Mary would find out soon enough she could not very well marry the man she loved and not his profession, especially since his profession was that of the Christian ministry. But she knew Mary well enough to know that Mary would be too sensible not to include his profession when she realized the two were harder to separate than to accept.

And so it was. As the happy couple day by day trod the marital pathway together, loving, honoring, and cherishing each other, Mary gradually found his profession a part of her life. Years passed. It was Sunday night; it had been a full day in the church for both Mary and the man she loved. They were seated in the breakfast nook munching a morsel before retiring, relaxing from the tenseness of the day and confiding to each other the deep joys of such service as they had been able to render.

It was Mary who spoke. "John, I've often laughed at a silly thing I said before we were married. It was this: I said, 'I'm marrying the man I love and not his profession,'—as though one could do such a thing! But if I married you again, I'd want you to have the same profession. It's just real fun working together in the church, isn't it?"

Many others have shared Mary's feeling before their marriage. She had no formal training for comradeship in her husband's profession. She had not studied systematic theology, nor homiletics, nor church management. Her college course was never planned with the slightest hint of preparing her to be a minister's wife. Even if she had known she would marry a young theologue, where would she have turned for a course designed especially for a minister's wife? In the seminaries she knew of, the special courses were planned for professional parish workers. And then every church is different, anyway.

Isn't it true that a successful minister's wife just fits in, using whatever training she has had? At any rate, that is what Mary thought after a group of ministers' wives had spent an afternoon together, telling what they did in their particular churches. None had had special training to become a minister's wife. They had been trained as teachers, musicians, nurses, secretaries, and what not. To her it seemed that they had used their good sense, their native ability, and the training they had; and, by some divine intuition, each had adapted herself to the needs of her church. Their training was a gradual and continuing process, a lifetime course, which had begun on the first Sunday in the husband's new charge and would extend, it seemed, to the day of his retirement.

If we should ask Mary, after her years of experience, what a minister's wife should do in the church, she would no doubt be quick to say, "That depends upon the church; for rural, town, and city churches vary in their demands upon the minister's wife as well as upon the minister. But fortunate is the minister's wife who is wise and versatile enough to see where she can best serve the church." But if pressed to be specific, Mary would probably bring out the following points.

In the first place, a congregation expects the wife of its minister to be a part of its fellowship. No matter how much she would like to worship in another church because of its worshipful architecture or its splendid music, or how much she would like to preserve her membership in her former church because of the many ties which bind, to do so would provoke unfavorable comment in the congregation. But it would be the exceptional minister's wife who would not want to become an active member of the church her husband serves. And she wants to be an ideal member.

As a church member, the minister's wife must set an example in reverence in the house of God, in promptness, and in attendance at the regular worship services and meetings of the church. At times she may long to remain at home; but aside from the personal rewards of regular attendance, she finds opportunity to touch the lives of others in the public service. Hence she goes to church; her friends and fellow members know she will be present—reverent, prompt, faithful.

To retain the custom of the family pew, which every minister desires for the families of his congregation, may at times be difficult for the minister's wife, but to do so is at least worth trying. This custom has been revived in some congregations by the example of the minister's family. Parents and children are drawn the closer together in the act of worshiping side by side.

There is not only a personal gain for the minister's wife in practicing the virtues her husband preaches, ever seeking to develop her own Christian character; there is also a blessing

28

for the congregation, who recognize in her life "the fruit of the spirit . . . . love, joy, peace, longsuffering, kindness, goodness, faithfulness, meekness, self-control."

The admonition of Paul that women keep silence in the church is not interpreted to apply to the modern Protestant church, judging from the public service of women today. The membership of the average church is approximately sixty per cent women and forty per cent men; naturally there is a place for the leadership of women. In fact, efficient leadership is the greatest need of the day, and women who can lead will find large tasks awaiting them. The minister's wife is usually a woman with a fair education and a degree of culture, and she more often than not possesses some ability for public work. She therefore faces a problem: As a Christian, a church member, and one at least partly trained, how fully should she assume leadership? The question is important because it is quite as much an art to know what not to do as what to do in the church.

It is difficult to establish an unchangeable rule for the duties of a minister's wife in the church, for the problems of the churches differ. The needs of the small struggling church may make it a necessity for her to head an organization or a department, whereas in some larger church it may be wholly unfair to the congregation for her to assume leadership. Willingness on her part to fill in or help out where needed and to give hearty co-operation to others who lead should be her attitude. Generally speaking, it would seem unwise for the minister's wife to be at the head of any organization in the church, for two reasons. First, she should have equal interest in the work of all organizations of the church, and this can hardly be done if she carries the responsibility of leadership in any one. Second, her concern should primarily be to develop leaders rather than to lead. This is even much harder than to lead. It is said to be easier to do the work of ten than to train ten to do the work; but, for the permanent good of a congregation, it is more rewarding to train the ten. Ministers are subject to a change of pastorates, and it is a great joy to return to a former field of work to find the work prospering and those one has trained carrying on faithfully. The wife of a minister often meets her most delicate situations in regard to assuming leadership in organizations; caution and tactfulness are always aids in meeting them. To be slow in suggesting changes until she has won the confidence of the membership comes within the rule of caution.

A minister's wife is of greatest value in developing leadership when she recognizes the necessity of growing in knowledge as well as in grace. Whatever her educational preparation prior to her marriage has been, as the wife of a minister she will find it of real worth to be a diligent student of the thought, life, and activity of both the local and the universal church. It is helpful to keep informed on the work of one's own denomination, to know denominational history and polity, to be familiar with the extent of the institutions and missionary activities of the denomination, to be acquainted with the denominational plans and programs of work issued by the several boards and other agencies of the church, to know where to secure resource materials available for the various groups in the church.

To help her to keep abreast of the demands of the day, the minister's wife has the opportunity to attend lectures, conventions, and conferences. There are also opportunities for development in her own home which other women in the congregation may not have, since she has access to religious books and magazines in her husband's library which may not be found in the average library. If she is to help those she has encouraged to lead, she will no doubt find it a good plan to keep a simple filing system, making notes of ideas gleaned here and there, clipping and marking items as she reads, filing materials for worship services, programs, social occasions, special days, community service, international relations, such as will be of help to women's, young people's, or children's organizations or projects. She has access to materials coming to a minister's home which others are not likely to receive. But she should beware! There must be no clipping of Husband's magazines until he has had a chance to look over them! The studious wife will make notations in the file for reference, rather than have him find a paragraph missing from an article in which he has a deep interest.

Teachers are needed in the present-day church with its Sunday school, its various programs of religious and missionary education, and its study groups. It is perhaps in this field that the minister's wife will find it possible to render the most needed service. The same principles, however, which apply to heading an organization apply to teaching as well. The difference lies in the fact that the average church has classes or groups enough to absorb all the available teaching leadership, especially in the smaller churches, so that the minister's wife is not so likely to be taking the place of another.

Wherever she may fit in as a teacher, her effort will be of greatest service when the work she does magnifies her Lord and the church, rather than herself. Thus the work can easily be transferred to another if need arises; or, if the opportunity presents itself, she may help to develop another leader in that particular sphere.

31

The experience of many suggests that the minister's wife, no matter how gifted for public work she may be, or what training she may have acquired, remember that she is still the wife and not the minister of the church. She may crave the opportunity to fill the pulpit, and she may even be a better public speaker than her husband; but if she desires him to succeed she will let him be the preacher. Even when her husband must be away from his pulpit for a Sunday or two, it would seem far better to secure a pulpit supply than to have the wife in any way appear as a rival of her husband. Even though she may be an ordained minister, she will find that she can still serve her husband best by letting him do the preaching.

It is fortunate if the minister's wife is a musician and has developed the fine art of appreciation of good church music, for she will find many occasions where she can be of help both to her husband and to the church. In this realm of service, as in other realms, seeking the limelight in the church might hinder her influence; whereas awaiting opportunities to fill in, with a spirit of willingness to help where there is need, seems a safe rule to follow. Often through the children's and young people's groups there is an opportunity for the minister's wife to help to develop in the congregation a real appreciation of good church music. To keep abreast of the new and fine things in music of a religious nature enables one to be ready with constructive suggestions when they are needed. Often need prompts the minister's wife to organize a choir or chorus of some particular age group in the church. If so, to turn over the work to others as soon as leadership is available is a good gesture in developing the future leadership of the congregation.

Using opportunities to speak words of appreciation and praise for the music of the church, when such can be sincerely given, is one avenue to encourage good music in the church. Or there may be occasion to offer criticism to organist or choir leaders or others. All such criticism should be tactful and constructive. Suggestions for helps and available resources for good music may be just what some leader is seeking.

The minister's wife is not hired by the church board to be a parish visitor, but her interest in her husband's work in each new parish seems to present anew the question of visitation. She finds that the churches differ, the rural church differing widely from the city church. The large city church may have its staff of paid workers, while the country church can afford neither parish visitor nor secretary. Each church presents a distinct field for study, but a few general facts apply to all.

If family duties permit her to do so, the wife may wish to accompany her husband on his first round of get-acquainted calls to learn to know the families of the parish. But most ministers would consider it unwise for their wives to accompany them in all of their calling. When a third party is present there is a restraint on the part of the parishioners who wish to speak to the minister of their personal problems, and the minister may likewise be timid in having them express their confidences. A thoughtful minister's wife will not want the parishioners denied because of her presence the privilege of opening their hearts to their spiritual adviser.

There are times and circumstances, however, when a minister will desire his wife to be with him when he calls. Such occasions are those of calling upon a woman who is confined to her bed by illness, especially in her home where there is no attending nurse, or upon some woman of doubtful character, or upon a neurotic woman who is apt to exaggerate or misconstrue the minister's personal interest in her.

A minister's wife usually has her own calling list. Her visits bring cheer to the lonely and the shut-ins, or they delight the young mother who has just come home from the hospital with her new first-born. The calls include neighborly visits, when she "just drops in." She may also find that she can be helpful to her husband by frequent use of the telephone, as in the case of continued illness, or by giving a friendly ring to find out why some faithful worshiper was absent. A democratic church appreciates the minister's wife who is democratic in her calling, including alike in her list both rich and poor, learned and unlearned, the indifferent and the faithful. A record of calls, noting circumstances and ailments told her by those upon whom she called, will aid her later in making inquiry concerning their well-being. Her record will help her husband also to show intelligent and sympathetic interest. But whatever is shared with her and her husband in confidence, they will, of course, seal within their hearts.

It is helpful to any minister if his wife too is acquainted with the membership of the church, for she will ofttimes see folk from a different angle from her husband's, and thus be able to give him a woman's viewpoint. But it is not easy! If the membership is large, it is difficult to know all the names and the faces; yet it is a worth-while effort to develop one's memory for names and one's ability to recognize people.

To learn to know the congregation, one minister's wife tried the plan of standing at one of the two exits of the church to shake hands with the departing worshipers, while her husband stood at the other. In the evening she and her husband reversed the order of standing at the doors. The comment on this procedure by an observer was, "More people found it necessary to leave through the exit over which she presided than

34

by the other door." This fact alone would make such a plan seem inadvisable, for it is well to bear in mind that there are attentions and functions which belong to the minister of the church and not to the minister's wife. The wife's standing at the exit to shake hands seems to savor of the professional and would be frowned upon by most congregations. It would be more pleasing to many to see her showing a friendly attitude in greeting those she meets, chatting a moment or two with a few who can be helped and cheered rather than shaking hands perfunctorily with many.

The minister's wife who is quick to recognize and greet strangers, irregular attendants, those back from a siege of illness, or those who may need words of encouragement is most generally appreciated. It is a good custom not to hurry away from a meeting, for tarrying to chat often gives an opportunity for a better acquaintance.

No matter what place of service the minister's wife may have in the church, her work will be greatly augmented if she has a vision of the larger fellowships of the Christian Church. As her husband seeks to interpret Christianity in its wider relations, she too may help those with whom she works to catch the vision of God's will for his world as one great fellowship of love and service; of the marvelous possibilities of Christianity as it may find expression through the various organizations and groups in the church and through the association of churches; of the value and the potential power of each small group as a part of a great Church Universal.

With such a vision, the parish of her husband's church will never seem small or limited, but a part of a great and ever enlarging force to help build a righteous world.

III

HER PRIVILEGES

GRACE TILTON SHULLENBERGER

MY OWN personal experience as a minister's wife has been one so full and rich and varied that I can think of no other profession my husband might have chosen which would have given me the opportunity to live so abundantly.

Anna French Johnson, in her book *The Making of a Minister's Wife,* says:

A man may be consecrated to the ministry from infancy, but the woman who shares his task just blunders into it, for of all the professions open to women that of the minister's wife offers the least formal training. She falls in love with and marries her young theologue, and thereby plunges without apprenticeship into a complicated, demanding institutional life. But her intensive training begins the day she becomes mistress of the manse, and it does not end until she and her minister husband retire to live on their modest pension.

Not long ago I was a guest at a club in another city in my state. Across from me at the luncheon table sat a woman who I soon learned was a retired minister's wife. She put to me this very pointed question: "Don't you get terribly tired going to meetings and being called upon unexpectedly to have the devotions, or to teach a class in Sunday school at the last minute?" And then she told me how the weight of responsibility had rolled from her shoulders the day her husband

36

retired. I think there must be a sense of freedom after thirty, forty, fifty years of service, when one shifts the responsibility to younger shoulders; but I think, too, that there must be a sense of great loss—a feeling that no longer you belong to a people who are part of your very being, with whom you have walked in the Valley of the Shadow, and with whom you have shared mountain-peak experiences.

A seminar for ministers' wives in connection with the pastors' Institute held each summer at the University of Chicago has been of great help to those of us who could attend. One of our leaders spoke these words of wisdom, "The greatest inducement to be a minister's wife is the minister himself." As I recall those days in our first pastorate together—and that is more than thirty years ago—one of the most precious memories of all is the way in which my husband's congregation received me into their hearts and their homes. The picture of that first reception, when the women brought to the church parlors their choicest possessions to make the occasion beautiful—their rugs, their draperies, the best of china and silver, flowers in profusion— that picture of the gracious hospitality of those people hangs on memory's wall for all time.

Very soon I learned that my husband had brought me to a life that was exacting, that called for tact and understanding and patience in double portion; but as I look back over the years and forward to the days ahead, I would not have him other than that which he chose to be.

The church wants to be proud of its minister and of his wife—justly proud of their consecration to the task to which they are called. I firmly believe that a great deal depends upon the minister's wife; she must help her husband grow in spiritual power and usefulness in his church, in the community, and in the brotherhood.

I wonder whether there is any other profession in which a man has so constantly to keep pace with the times, in his reading, in his study, and in his interest in world-wide affairs. A minister's wife must do without many things in order that her husband may buy books. If it's a new rug—and somehow the rugs of the manse have a way of wearing so thin—or a particular set of encyclopedias—well, there is never a question. The books are purchased and duly installed. As the minister fingers the pages and loses himself in contemplation, his wife sits quietly, with a bit of mending, glancing occasionally across the room, and ponders, as her fingers fly faster and faster, on how she can make the old rug hold out for another year. My "Webster's Unabridged" informs me that an encyclopedia is a work in which various branches of knowledge are discussed; but I've looked in vain, hours on end, for information on how to help three pairs of busy little feet and hands drag fire engines and trains across a floor without disturbing father in his search for knowledge.

The editor of one of our church journals conceived the idea of a series of articles by children of the manse on the theme, "My Dad—Preacher, Pastor, Person." A young man asked to write of his father chose the subject, "My Minister Is Also My Father." An arresting paragraph reads thus:

Another picture of my father is simple in content and setting— yet it is characteristic of him and has exercised a profound influence upon me and upon my brothers. He is sitting in a comfortable chair surrounded by bright light from an adjacent reading lamp. He is reading a book, his attitude relaxed, yet studious and atten- tive. This regard for reading and study is a thing I have admired and tried to cultivate in myself. I know that most of his success in the pulpit and in public appearance has been made possible by a cultural background, prepared and maintained all his life by the feeling toward knowledge of a student rather than a teacher.

I am sure there is not one of us who doesn't want her husband to be a great preacher—a man who feeds the souls of his people as he comes before them each Lord's Day. If he is to be that sort of man, his own soul must first be fed. The prayers of ministers' wives that their husbands may speak words of helpfulness and encouragement and inspiration to those who come to worship form a golden pathway to the throne of grace.

In addition to his reading and his study, the minister must attend and must have a part in religious gatherings. The churches from the beginning have made it a practice to meet in conference where questions of the moment are discussed. Every church ought to make it possible for its minister to go to state and national church conventions. He needs the inspiration of other voices and the fellowship of his brother ministers. Many a time I have shed bitter tears because I couldn't attend these meetings with my husband. It is often true that there are not sufficient funds for both, and, again, the home and family must be cared for. A challenge it is, to the mistress of the budget, to get the minister himself there.

There's no time for weeping if the minister's wife keeps up with her husband's interests; for she too must find time for reading, and for her music, if that has been a special part of her training. Whatever talent she may possess, it should be her privilege and her duty to develop it in the way that keeps her physically and mentally at her best, for thus she is able to serve efficiently in the home and in the church.

A dear friend, the successful wife of a successful minister, when asked what she considered the greatest virtue or characteristic needed by the minister's wife, replied, "I should say unhesitatingly: poise and gumption." If in the midst of a daily routine that calls for administration, organization, and program building, she cannot move with serenity among the women of her church, and in addition preside over her home with poise and confidence, her greatest usefulness is lost.

There is one saving grace every minister and his wife should foster—a sense of humor. They need it in the home and they need it in abundance in the church. Many serious situations have been met and solved by a sense of humor. Salvation from defeat and despair is often brought about by a bit of fun.

Every minister's wife should have on the bookshelf of her own room a copy of Cora Harris' book *The Circuit Rider's Wife,* and the companion to it, *The Circuit Rider's Widow.* Human nature hasn't changed from the day of the circuit rider to this. Again and again, I have thumbed through the pages of Mrs. Harris' books and laughed and wept with the author in her delineation of characters one finds in every congregation.

What activities to undertake each lady of the manse must work out for herself. One spoke to a group of ministers' wives at our International Church Convention. She began thus: "Ministers' wives—and having so addressed you, may we put the appellation aside while for a brief time we think of ourselves as the *favored laywomen* of the church."

For right or wrong we know that the church does expect more of the minister's wife than of other laywomen. But as it places responsibility it helps also toward accomplishment. The task is never too hard. The acceptance or rejection of this truth determines whether the life of the minister's wife will be a long series of irritations or of welcome opportunities to build altars that will take her nearer to God.

As the minister's wife, am I by my attitudes helping or hindering my husband in his great task of Kingdom building? Am I always charitable with those who disagree with me? Am I interested in developing a better feeling among women of different denominations? Am I helping the youth of our day to find the high road of Christian living? Am I giving guidance to young men and young women who have taken the vow to "love, cherish, care for, and keep sacred each one the other so long as they both shall live," helping them to find in the church a "noble anchor" for that new home? Am I talking, praying, working with all Christian women for the day when the fatherhood of God, and the brotherhood of man will become a reality among all the peoples of the earth?

After all is said and done, I wonder whether the best guide for our lives is not found in these verses from Proverbs:

> Strength and dignity are her clothing; . . . .
> She openeth her mouth with wisdom;
> And the law of kindness is on her tongue.
> She looketh well to the ways of her household,
> And eateth not the bread of idleness.
> Her children rise up and call her blessed;
> Her husband also, and he praiseth her.

IV

HER OPPORTUNITIES

GEORGIANA SIBLEY GLENN

WHILE SPENDING the years from 1930 to 1940 in a college town, my minister husband and I noticed a tremendous change in the attitude of the graduating students about their life work. At first all expected to make enough money to retire in early middle age, but as the decade wore on there came an increasing desire to devote their lives to improving the condition of the nation and of the world. Young men were studying for the foreign service, not because they wanted to wear white spats, but because they felt it was a method of improving international relations. They were studying law, not to find rich clients but to work at the legal framework for social reconstruction. They looked for jobs in connection with the League of Nations, not because of the interest of foreign travel but in the hope of strengthening the ties which bind the world together. Politics and government service became a crusade for the strong rather than a fixed salary for the weak.

Even those studying architecture were concerned with low-cost housing. Some went into broadcasting stations and newspaper offices, feeling that this was the most effective way of educating public opinion; and many in the business courses were seriously thinking of business as their way of improving the economic conditions of their fellow citizens. President Lowell's description of business as "the oldest of the arts and the newest of the professions" began to be realized.

The thing that interested us, a rectory family, in all this was that it seldom occurred to these young men that the ministry had a more direct influence upon social change than had any other profession or position. They would say quite bluntly, "I believe in God, but I want to spend my life working for this world, not the next." They conceived the job of a minister as working for the church, quite forgetting that the church is its people. They thought that the minister does not have time to understand the forces which are changing our outlook, not realizing that only the minister is fortunate enough to spend his entire time studying causes and working for a better world. They felt that the minister was looked on by outstanding people as sincere but futile, never having noticed that intelligent, alert, able ministers are to be found taking leadership in every progressive movement.

If these idealistic students did not realize the place of the minister as an inspirer of social action, it is natural that people in general have not realized the opportunities that come to his wife. The minister's wife is a very fortunate person if she is really concerned with this changing world, and the church's place in it. With a minimum of effort on her part she has an opportunity to know a great many people of various opinions and to know them well. Whether she deserves it or not, people look on her as a friend; they take her concern for them and their way of life as something to be expected, and they are often terrifyingly willing to take her advice. The minister's wife goes in and out of the homes of the rich and of the poor. She knows the young people who come from her church homes, conservative and liberal. She may well have a chance to guide these young people in activities and thinking, and most parents are inclined to consider her guidance wise.

It is evident that I am speaking of the minister's wife who is interested in the work of the church—not only because it is her husband's profession and life, but also because she cares about it and feels able and willing herself to work for the advancement of God's reign upon earth. I am sympathetic with the minister's wife who feels she married a man and not a church, although I would find it difficult to separate the two, so enthusiastic is my husband about his work. I understand too the wife who has all she can handle in making a home for her husband and children. She has a special contribution to make in a changing world; she provides a haven of unchanging affection.

But I do not feel that inactive wives of the clergy have any particular "place" in the world—that is, any place different from that of other wives and mothers. The world does give a "place" to those who choose to claim it by working for it; it is especially generous in the place it gives to the minister's wife, but she must prove she deserves it.

The activities of the minister's wife are the same as those of other conscientious churchmen. The work among the people within the parish who are learning to live as Christians is a large one. The church is, after all, made up of people in various stages of religious development. But all turn to the church for strength and leadership. In these times of change it represents the things that stand fast. No matter what uncertainties we face as individuals and as a nation and a world, there are certainties which are eternal. "God cares," says the church; "underneath are the everlasting arms." Stability in a world where so much seems unstable is the greatest thing we can give to young and old.

The minister's wife is one of those in the church to whom

the people look when things are especially uncertain. If she has truly given herself to doing God's work, she feels, and so do the people she works with, that it is the church, not a particular individual, which is caring for them. This is of primary importance. In order really to help people in moments of spiritual and emotional uncertainty we must teach them to find for themselves the source of power which can continue to strengthen them until they in turn can help others.

If the minister's wife feels herself an instrument for service, there are many times when she can be used. In the first place, she can do a great deal of the actual research and follow-up work in connection with parishioners who are having health or home or financial difficulties. Many women will talk more freely to a woman, and most of us women are more patient than our husbands in listening to details. Where there are children involved, too, a woman is often more experienced. But, most important of all, she can save her husband a great deal of time by taking routine activities off his shoulders.

A great deal of the work of the church is with well-adjusted and interested parishioners. The minister's wife sees much of them through calling and inviting them to her home, and through meetings. But she believes that everyone, even the least well-adjusted and the least attractive, has something to contribute to the life of the church.

People on the outside often say to me, "How can you stand the boring and difficult people who work in church organizations?" The obvious answer is that most people have appealing qualities when you get to know them and that many who at first sight seem unattractive often show such devotion, unselfishness, and real beauty of character that they are appealing through sheer goodness. But a less obvious and also

45

important answer to the same question is, "What, then, is the task of the church? Is it not to take misfits and through love and patience teach them to fit, to endure the society of selfish souls while they learn unselfishness, to be patient with the proud who have not discovered the sweetness of humility, to care for the lonely when they need it most?" If the church is too busy for these people, it is indeed too busy. We must learn to think of each person as a potential legion for God. In a changing world it is important for each one to belong somewhere, to feel valuable and appreciated. The minister's wife has many opportunities to help people to find their niches.

On the other hand it is important to take care that no one who is taking his first steps in the life of the church is hurt by any of the so-called "difficult" people. The children of light must be clever in this generation; they must work to make the program of the church organizations challenging to all people, its activities of real interest and value in the community. Often the minister's wife can help to start new organizations to hold or stimulate the interest of those who are not active in the already functioning groups. We should be realistic in our approach. For example, some women like to sew and give valuable "needle hands" to the sewing circle; others just don't like sewing, but can offer different gifts and abilities. The church must look at the people first, their needs, their interests, the time they have free, and then develop organizations which will serve them and in which they can serve. The minister's wife has her part in this and also often has an opportunity to integrate the work of different organizations and to guide their thinking about what their special contributions can be. Church organizations must become wider channels of usefulness. From time to time the minister's wife can help to widen these channels.

Some ministers' wives—I am one of this number—are especially interested in the training of young people. A leading Canadian educator has said, "There has been in education too much to question and to doubt, too little in which to believe and trust." Young people today, sensing the uncertainties of their parents and their teachers, begin to wonder if there is anything in which they can believe or trust. In our tolerance we have, during the last twenty years, often given the impression that it not only did not matter what one believed, but also did not matter whether one believed anything at all. Young people are asking us to become articulate in these terrible times—to state what it is we cherish, for what we would be willing to suffer and sacrifice. We answer: human liberty, freedom to serve God, the rights of each citizen, the value of every individual. If they should say, "We are dying for these aims; what is the organization that is living for them?" we can proudly and truthfully say, "The Church!"

If we would hold the interest and loyalty of our young people, we must make progress in our religious education. To do so requires, partly, well-planned Sunday school; partly, where possible, weekday religious education; partly weekday organizations, church or Boy or Girl Scouts, where the attitudes emphasized on Sundays are put to the test; partly, young people's groups for discussion, for social contact, for service. Whatever the organization, it must be advised and led by an adult who sees in each child the possibility of growing in favor with God and man, who knows how to put first things first, and who has a sense of humor.

Some ministers' wives like to work at all this. The most

rewarding part of my career as a minister's wife has been my work with the young people who came into our home to share their triumphs or problems or sorrows—to talk of the team they didn't make, the mother who can't see their point of view, the leading part they were given in the school play. These same young people came back later on the verge of eloping or when they had got into trouble or had been shocked by death for the first time. Each visit from them has given me a new opportunity to help them. And they, have helped me. I am eternally grateful that I am a minister's wife and therefore their friend.

So far I have written only of the minister's wife in the parish. But the parish is not the world, and the alert minister's wife finds herself led into activities not limited by parish concerns.

I was interested in helping my older parish girls to get summer jobs as mother's helpers, in order to help them financially and to give them a summer home. With this in mind, I organized a course to teach them the fundamentals of child care, housecleaning, easy laundry work, answering the telephone, simple waiting on the table, and neat appearance. Soon many people wanted to engage my girls. As a result of this effort I became much interested in the high school and other courses in domestic science for training household workers available in the city, in the situation in which many household workers lived, and in their health conditions. Everyone with whom I came in contact in this study, from the mayor and the school principals to the clinical doctors and the household employers, took it perfectly for granted that, as a minister's wife, I should be concerned with my girls and other girls, their jobs and their happiness. I needed to give no explana-

V

HER WIDER OUTLOOK

WINIFRED MEAD CLINCHY

MY EDUCATION in good will among the various religious groups into which the world seems to be divided has been a gradual and withal delightful process. My path has taken me to pleasant places in the yards of churches other than my own. Indeed, the total number of friendships my husband and I have formed beyond the borders of our denomination exceeds the sum of the warm friends we have in the circle of our church. On the basis of our experiences, we would encourage every minister and his wife to develop acquaintances with the leaders and people of all religious and racial cultures of our nation.

The example and pattern were set for me in childhood. In the home of my Methodist minister father, men and women of many races and many Protestant religious denominations dined at our table and were entertained in our home. I am sure that my feeling of interest in and appreciation of the Negro people and problems grew out of what I could understand of the conversations among prominent Negro leaders who were often in our home. But, as I remember it, the associations were largely among Methodists, both preachers and lay people. I was conscious that there were other Protestant groups, but until my high school years I did not know much about them. There was never any antagonism expressed toward other evangelical peoples, but there was not much intercourse even between the various Protestant ministers of the period.

51

Then, when I was in college, World War I came. My father was sent to France with a group of Y.M.C.A. workers. They were men of all denominations; and, in the course of that war service, men of all faiths came very close together. Catholic priests, Jewish rabbis, and Protestant ministers co-operated. That experience, I observed, broadened my father's outlook in respect to the religious beliefs outside the Protestant group. Afterwards he associated himself with people of all religious faiths and was respected and loved by many people of every group, all over this country.

During the war, I married a young officer who later entered the Presbyterian ministry. In the course of his theological training, which came after our marriage, I learned many things about various religious traditions. Until that time, even though I had had a college education, "comparative religions" had meant little to me.

The Ku Klux Klan was flourishing in the little country parish where we lived from 1919 to 1923, and for the first time in my life I saw decent people completely carried away by an ugly emotional experience which seemed to be totally foreign to their usual considerate and kindly lives. I heard the things which, although lies, were repeated by people who considered themselves truthful citizens. I saw things done to innocent Negroes, and helpless Jews and ostracized Catholics which were bewildering to me. Fortunately, I was spared some of the horrors which did actually take place during that strange period after the war. But the experience made my husband and me begin to ask, How do people get that way? What makes otherwise civilized people react to a social situation with harshness and even brutality?

In 1923 our home became the religious work center of the

College Church and Christian Association at Wesleyan University in Middleton, Connecticut. It has been estimated that I baked fifteen thousand waffles for hungry students in four interesting years. It was lots of fun, but the important angle is that those waffles strengthened Catholic and Jewish boys just as they did the Methodist and Presbyterian majorities. We discovered a curious truth: when Protestants sat around a fireside with Catholic priests and rabbis of distant synagogues, they became better Protestants. That is no reflection on the priests and rabbis; the point is that each boy was forced to think through the values and the practices of his own upbringing. A student usually became more intelligent about his own faith, and more sympathetically reverent toward the reverences of others.

One winter we held a parley on religion. It was as popularly attended as a basketball game or a college prom. Rabbi Stephen S. Wise, Father John Cooper, Dr. William Adams Brown, Dr. John Haynes Holmes, and even a doubting agnostic professor from another college were the leaders. It made a more lasting impression than any revival I have ever known.

In 1928 we had the opportunity to put some of our theories to work on a broader scale. The Federal Council of the Churches of Christ in America was very much disturbed about religious prejudice and persecution. Several years earlier they had formed a committee, entirely of Protestants—the Ku Klux Klan was an exclusively Protestant affair!—to see what could be done to immunize Americans against hate. A committee on good will worked for four years. After some experimentation, Dr. S. Parkes Cadman, Justice Charles Evans Hughes, and others established a National Conference of Protestants, Catholics and Jews. My husband was selected to direct the program. From that time on, my life has traversed fascinating crossroads.

A young girl brought up in a parsonage does not usually have the opportunity to meet religious leaders of the "outside" religious groups. And that word "outside" is exactly what I mean. I do not believe that in my early youth I thought Catholics were quite normal, and certainly I never associated the present-day Jews with the life of Jesus. That is significant, for never in my Sunday school training was the present-day American Jew considered important enough even to be related to the killing of Jesus. I have found in recent years that Jewish religious leaders feel that the Christian child gets his hatred of the Jew from the story of Christ's crucifixion. That may be, but it was never brought out anywhere in my early religious training.

Suddenly, in my husband's work, I was associating not only with Catholic and Jewish people but with the religious leaders of both groups. Curiously enough, I am sure my parents were worried for fear my own religious convictions and those of my husband would be corrupted if not completely destroyed in this association with other groups. As I talked to Catholic priests and Jewish rabbis, I found that they were really as human in their interests and outlook and as earnest in their faith as the Protestants I had heard talk around my father's table. There came a time when I first began to wonder where all these prejudices which we now talk about had received their start.

I adventured into comparative religions enough to get some background for the discussions my husband and his friends were having. And my laboratory work was the most valuable kind a student can have. I learned to know and understand the thoughts of Catholic clergy and their ambitions for their work. I can remember that I was *shocked* when I first heard a Catholic nun laugh. I had thought, because of their celibate life of sacrifice and their unusual garb, that nuns had given up all their normal friendly intercourse with people and their interest in what was going on in the world. This may all seem childish, but I have found it was not only my experience but that of many other Protestant women whom I later heard talk at conferences of the three predominent faiths, Catholic, Jewish, and Protestant, held in many parts of the United States. A sense of surprise is revealed in exclamations such as, "Hasn't Sister Mary the loveliest hands!" or, "Why, her idea on the education of children is exactly what I have been saying for years!" A sense of embarrassment usually precedes the acceptance of an invitation to lunch with a Catholic priest. Time and time again I have had guests say to me, "I shall be pleased to come, of course, but I have never eaten at a table with a priest. What must I talk about?"

All of these experiences were mine in the beginning, and to find that most of my Protestant friends have the same reactions has convinced me that my early training was not unusual, although perhaps it was more kindly than the average. Occasionally an invitation of mine is refused because the guest must talk to or sit beside a Catholic priest or Jewish rabbi, but those occasions are getting fewer and fewer. The common, everyday association between women in clubs and civic organizations in the last twenty years has made much easier the task of creating better understanding among different groups.

And yet the social cleavage, if such it can be called, goes very deep, and appears in unexpected places. I have known many women, for instance, who work actively beside women of other religious groups in welfare work and yet cannot bring themselves to invite these same women into their homes unless with the tacit understanding that they will not assume therefore to consider themselves "friends." I am being very frank, but I am anxious to recognize the fact that some of these feelings and prejudices run deeper than we realize. It is perhaps intellectually that we first win our battle for understanding people who are different from ourselves. Our emotional attitudes lag far behind. One very good friend of mine, helpful and co-operative where interfaith work is concerned, said to me one day, "Intellectually I know that the Negroes you introduce me to are as fine as any friends I may have, but it would make me sick at my stomach to sit down to a meal with them." Her upbringing in the South had conditioned her emotional life to a degree hard to control. My husband's background is Protestant Scotch-Irish; and his father, tolerant in most things, has a very hard time comprehending my husband's understanding of the Catholics—again a question of background. I have friends who have had unpleasant experiences with a Jewish merchant, let us say, and invariably will insist that all Jewish people are tricky. Our tendency to lump people together can become a very grave danger in these times. We would be insulted if, in a similar fashion, a sweeping judgment were passed upon us as "Protestants" together with some people of a different temper who also belong to the Protestant group.

It has taken time, I will have to admit, for me to become sensitive to the best in the people belonging to groups outside my own. I remember my first association with the Mormon group. I made the acquaintance of a young Mormon missionary at college, and my family was much concerned about it. A few years ago I was entertained in a charming home in a Western city, where the host and his sister were children of a plural marriage, children of sisters who had married one man and had lived very happily. The marriages, of course, had taken place many years before; but I must confess that I was puzzled because there was no sense of apology on the part of my hosts. I had never been told the better side of the picture of the Latter Day Saints. And I might have gone on in my ignorance, if my mind had not been changed and my emotions reconditioned by personal, understanding intercourse with these friendly people.

I have been especially fortunate in having been able to travel in various countries of the world, with the object of interviewing the leaders of the various religious groups in these countries. The scenery and other beauties of the Old World have been a sort of backdrop for interesting personalities rather than objects of interest in themselves. I have been entertained in the charming home of one of the monsignors of the Roman Catholic Church in his apartment on the Place Venezia, across from Mussolini's headquarters. There, with only Catholic priests as hosts to my husband and me, I heard discussed, from the church point of view, the training of Italian youth. Under such circumstances, the differences between the Catholic and Protestant clergy faded into the background. We have been entertained by the Jewish leader in Warsaw, when the medium of communication was a few words in broken English on his part and a few words in German on ours. I can remember the experience, as if it were today, of sitting with this gentleman of the former Polish Senate in the official box at the opera, the theme of which was the story of Napoleon's invasion of Poland. Under such circumstances, society's distinctions between Jew and Gentile are forgotten.

You may suppose that all my associations with these other groups have been pleasant. Most of them have been so, but some have not. The same variety exists also in experiences within my own traditional group. The pushing, loud, and vulgar woman at the bargain counter is not typical of any single class or race. My daughter sold stockings in a New York department store during the prewar rush for silk stockings, and her account of women and their peculiar behavior showed clearly that we have no foundation for certain generalizations spoken about the Jews. The dirtiest home I was ever in belongs to a family of good old Puritan stock which has not even the excuse of extreme poverty.

The years I have spent in close association with my husband's work has made me value *individuals,* for their charm and courtesy, thoughtfulness and generosity. I am not talking about the people of so-called education and refinement, although of course many, of varying racial backgrounds and religious affiliations, have had such advantages. My memories include warm and happy pictures of the little Italian peasant woman, who invited two wandering trampers into her spotless home in a small town in Italy; of the dirty Russian drayman in the city of Leningrad who wanted us to take his picture with our camera, and then send him a copy, in return for which he would carry us anywhere on his wagon; of the Syrian in Damascus who refused a tip for a favor done for two interested Americans; of the rancher in Montana who helped us fix a tire and discussed ranching with us. I could string together an endless chain of such recollections, and so could each of us. And yet our tendency is to label entire groups of strangers as "Bohunks," "Wops," "Kikes," "Greasers," "Micks." Once a Catholic confided, "Some of us call you 'Protestant pups'!" Innumerable are the names we have for each other to express our dislike for the unlike, for those we do not understand.

I have been very fortunate in that, before I am old enough, if one ever is, to have my likes and dislikes frozen into certain molds, I have been brought into happy association with people of every nationality, race, and creed the world over. Through this laboratory experience, I am gradually learning, intellectually and also emotionally, to understand why people are as they are and why they act as they do. I know that most people are not so fortunate in their selection of laboratories, but each of us lives in a community which is sure to include a cross section of American life. If we can be lifted out of our own little ingrown group and into the brotherhood of the community as a whole, I am sure the experience of many people can be like my own.

Our country is now at war with other nations. Our thought patterns will begin to freeze into certain molds of loyalty to one group on the one side, and hatred of another group on the other side. After this struggle is over and disillusionment sets in, with its accompaniment of unsettled economic conditions, the *hate* movements may start all over again; and our emotions, tired as they are after a war experience, will not vigorously withstand rumor and rancor. If we can only immunize ourselves now, while we are working side by side in the Red Cross and civilian defense organizations! Now is the time, while the economic strain is not desperate and while the sons of us all are side by side in the army camps. If we can attain a degree of understanding of the aims, ideas, and ideals of the groups not our own, then the hate movements will have no fertile ground in which to plant their seed, and hate will not germinate or grow. This country of ours cannot exist "half slave and half free"; and the slavery of hatred which is sweeping Europe and Asia today must not get a foothold here, or our democracy will perish.

VI

HER SPIRITUAL LIFE

LILLIAN DIEBOLD POLING

THE SUCCESSFUL Christian family is a true democracy. Here one should learn self-control, self-respect, honor, and chivalry, and the virtues of honesty, unselfishness, and sportsmanship. When the Christian home fails at any of these points, the failure is seldom made up for by any other agency. Here is the heart of the mission of the minister's wife, and here too is the permanent text from which her husband, if he is to be successful, must preach.

I am the twelfth and last child of my mother, who was a radiant Christian. Next to her home, she gave first place to her Saviour, to the church, to the minister and his family. I realize now what a large contribution she made to my life in the positions that I have been called upon to fill. And may I say at the very beginning that if I had all the possible choices in the world to consider or reconsider, I would choose now to be the wife of a minister.

A rugged mountain rises before the minister's wife, but as comrade and helpmate she finds her climb a joyous one. Hers is a path that leads to understanding and peace. With the man of her choice, she invests her life and does her bit to realize the Kingdom of God on the earth. She marries a minister because she loves him, if her motive is worthy. Then she finds herself in what is, I believe, the most important position open to womanhood anywhere in the world. Its opportunities and

60

responsibilities—yes, and its joys—far exceed her dreams. Such has been my experience.

Always there is in the heart of a true woman the mother instinct, which if developed and educated enriches and glorifies the greatest vocation open to woman—motherhood. This is true whether a woman mothers her own children, or the children of another, or the children of a community, or perhaps the childhood of a cause. Always the supreme instinct of womanhood is motherhood. And how repaid is a mother, how rewarded is a minister's wife for the love and care she lavishes upon her children! I have found the return on that investment large and continuing.

One afternoon late in August in a New England farmhouse, a letter came to my desk which had in it the call of a nominating committee, asking me to accept the presidency of the Council of Women for Home Missions. I was both amazed and honored. Who was I to assume so large and important a responsibility? My husband, of course, was the first to know, and in his generous and confident way he said, "Why not? The children are almost grown now, and your responsibilities in a parish are over for the present." He had just resigned a New York pastorate to give all his time to a youth program and to the editorial responsibilities of a religious journal. "Yes, why not?" he repeated.

As always in such matters, the family council, consisting of the five older children of our eight, was consulted. We called the council "The Family Round Table." After talking over possible duties and responsibilities and the home situation, the children also looked at me and said, "Why not, Mother?" They must all be in school, and we would be living in a New York hotel. So, after conferences with the chairman and members of the nominating committee, having the comforting assurance that a girlhood friend had assumed the executive secretaryship of the Council, and guided by many intimate conversations with the Heavenly Father, who himself seemed to open the door of opportunity, I accepted.

My years as a minister's wife had given me the opportunity to study the church intimately. I had felt the pulse of the women of the church and realized their problems and needs. Surely a New York downtown congregation and parish is one of the greatest mission fields in all the world, for the world passes that door, if it does not cross the threshold. My heart warms as I think of the friendship and love that, with hard tasks, were mine during those blessed years when I served as the wife of a pastor. Those memories will last forever.

With the new relationships, I came to a new perspective for church work and fellowship. Now I was a member of the congregation. I could feel as the woman feels who works without leadership responsibilities in the great missionary tasks of the whole church. On the Interdenominational Council I had my part with loyal women who gave of their time unstintingly and honored me with their support through happy years.

One of the most important things the Council of Women for Home Missions accomplished in that particular period was the further development of the World Day of Prayer. The beginning had been twenty-five years before in the vision of a gracious Christian woman who was the first president of the Council. Little did she think that her brave beginning would be magnified to its present far-reaching influence.

The World Day of Prayer became my special interest. Realizing that much more than had been done could be accomplished, and feeling that New York City was not aware of this significant opportunity, a few loyal persons met one Monday in a midcity hotel room. We met for prayer and consultation. We asked ourselves and the Heavenly Father that a way might be opened to a yet larger ministry for this unique, inspired plan. We believed that the world about us had not been roused to the power and resourcefulness of supplication and intercession. We sought God's care and encouragement, his guidance. And on that day there came into our hearts the knowledge that we did not so much need to know more about prayer as we did need to take time to pray together, as we did need to achieve a unity of prayer life across the continents and around the world. Thus began a program, a weekly prayer circle. We gathered each Monday, inviting others to join us. How many of those prayers were answered! How much was accomplished in that year! How filled with meaning did my own prayer life become!

Near the end of my third and last year as president of the Council, it was my privilege to accompany my husband on a visitation around the world. As opportunity permitted on this journey, I studied to discover how we might encourage the World Day of Prayer program so that it would indeed reach the uttermost places and persons. It was my privilege to meet with the missionaries and talk with them. Together we felt the call of a closer fellowship, and gladly they added to their plans our Monday worship service, which is now a continuing experience in at least twenty-five countries. There is no special organization; there is no pressure propaganda. There is the knowledge that our Heavenly Father knows that each Monday time is set aside for special attention to prayer, and that women far and near are praying to know the will and presence of the Holy Spirit.

It was intensely interesting to receive the reactions and testimonies of missionaries in far-off stations. Many of them were not able to assemble with their friends, save on this day. Now they realized that at home in their home churches their friends were praying for them—praying that they might have strength to meet their need. What it did for them, what I saw in their eyes as we talked, more than ever convinced me that the prayer fellowship, even with vast distances separating one from another, gives wisdom and power found nowhere else, courage and understanding to live for Christ and to serve his cause.

After six years, and following our return from this memorable trip, my schedule was again changed, as my husband was called to the pastorate of another downtown church, a church in Philadelphia. I knew now that one of the most vital contributions I could make as the minister's wife would be to organize a Fellowship of Prayer in the local congregation. We began with five women. Frequently now we have sixty or even eighty and more present. Always we have the presence of the Great Companion. Always we are conscious of his interest in us and in our problems. Always, though often not as we had sought, our prayers are answered; and, beyond all our hopes, our church has been blessed.

We meet each Monday afternoon in the home of the pastor. What an opportunity and privilege for the minister's wife! She must be something to everyone. Kindness and love must be hers, and prayer is the strength of her spirit and the meeting place for all her interests in others.

The unique power of prayer has been demonstrated by faithful Christians since Christ first taught his disciples the immortal prayer beginning "Our Father." If ever prayer fails to make a difference in our lives, we must admit, I think, that something in us is lacking, something that may be supplied. Perhaps a lack of faith or a failure to persevere has hindered us. From prayer so many have risen in triumph that this law of Christian living cannot be disproved.

> O Thou, by whom we come to God,
>   The Life, the Truth, the Way;
> The path of prayer Thyself hast trod,
>   Lord, teach us how to pray.

Always Jesus achieved by prayer, finding strength in a quiet place where he spoke to his Heavenly Father and received from God wisdom and power. This is the course we must take if we would make progress in our lives, if we would win the joy of our fellowship with Christ. How often the minister's wife needs courage to see things through! How often prayer helps her to a stronger faith! Robert Louis Stevenson, baffled and beaten with ill health, dying on a South Sea Island, could yet say because of his prayer life, "I believe in an ultimate decency of things." The minister's wife, praying, can understand that.

It is not easy to see things through. Perhaps any one of us could fight *one* brave battle all alone. Surely anyone can be good for *one* brief day, and anyone should be able to do *one* conspicuously unselfish thing in a lifetime. The hard thing is to live bravely in the everyday, day-after-day experiences. Life is a series of ever-increasing ordeals and struggles, and can be brought to a victorious conclusion only by enduring. The power to endure rises from the love of Jesus Christ, grows in the love of a great cause, and loses itself in the tasks of Christ's triumph. That power comes in prayer.

Perhaps you have felt and would say to me, "You have spoken of a sincere desire to know God through Jesus Christ.

65

That of itself would take a faith substantial enough to go forward and find this power." Many people say, perhaps carelessly and without serious thought, "I believe in God. I have faith in a God who rules this universe, but I cannot go further than that. To me personally he means nothing." But you may have a personal faith in a personal God. If such a faith does not give you a sense of security when in trouble, then you are missing power that is definitely available to you. It is faith in God, God as personal and individual, that makes us able to share, in a little at least, his power. Prayer is the fixing of our spiritual gaze in confidence upon the face of the Father.

Certainly a minister's wife must have faith in herself, faith in her husband, faith in her fellows, and, most of all, faith in God. Such a required, comprehensive faith can be attained only by prayer, through the experience, I may say, of *constant prayer*. Paul tells us that "faith is the substance of things hoped for, the evidence of things not seen." Often I need to repeat to myself those words—scientifically accurate! comforting to the soul! spiritually uplifting!

But James is also right: "Faith without works is dead." Realistic and true are these words. Faith becomes a propagating power only as it is harnessed in action. Often we take faith too much for granted. Occasionally we return to the words of James just to emphasize the need of works, as though faith were a simple matter but works more difficult. Faith alone is insufficient, but here is only a part truth. Great and good works are impossible without a great faith. Desire, purpose, and faith walk hand in hand. A great faith is not easy, but it grows as we set to work, as we seek to give faith expression. And surely these days are a challenge to personal as well as public works.

One night after a service in our own church, a young woman

came to ask whether she might bring to me a question, whether I would help her with her problem and advise her in a personal decision. She said that she was alone in New York, that she had been keeping company with a young man for about a year, and that now he had asked her to marry him. "But," she added, "he makes fun of the church and will never attend with me. I am a Christian. I keep my daily devotions and believe with all my heart in the Church of Jesus Christ. This young man is upstanding, with no bad habits. I love him, but he will have nothing to do with that which means everything in my life. What should be my answer?"

Surely, no young woman could face a more difficult problem. I, the minister's wife, replied, "My dear, I am unable to make your decision. I do not know the young man. But I trust you, and I would trust your judgment as to what should be done now. When you make your decision, when after earnest prayer —and I shall pray earnestly for you—you reach your conclusion, I shall be glad to help you. And always remember that when two people really love each other, each will be considerate of that which is precious to the other."

Three weeks passed, and then one Sunday evening the young woman appeared again. She came to me with these words: "I can't live without him. I do love him, and he loves me. But he will not make the decision to come to the church—now. He does respect my convictions now. What shall I do?"

I could only tell her that her decision seemed made, but that before her marriage there should be a definite understanding as to the things of her Christian faith that were to her vital. I advised that one real test would be setting up a family altar.

"But how," she replied, "could I do that? He would laugh at me, even if he allowed it."

I answered, "You have been accustomed to reading the Bible and praying before retiring. Then continue to do that. The Heavenly Father will help if you try. I shall pray with you that you may succeed in winning this man you love and that, as he loves and trusts you, he may follow you into the Christian life and into the church." I felt justified in assuring her that her love and faith would be rewarded.

She went away, saying that she would take my advice and that she would let me know.

Six months passed, and then came a letter. In it the young woman described how that morning, which was Easter Sunday, she and her husband, in their new home city, had joined the church together. Of course, I was very happy, and I was eager to know just how her experience developed. She wrote how difficult it was for him to understand at first, but that gradually his interest was stirred, that when first she read the Bible he would wait in silence, but that presently he wished her to read aloud. Then the letter told how step by step in those first blessed days of their life together, she was able to lead him to Christ.

It is such experiences as this that enrich the life of a minister's wife. The problems of human beings everywhere become her problems. She must meet them with respect. She must be a very understanding person, a tactful and a helpful person. She must get the viewpoint of other people, seeing things through their eyes. Yet again and again she must seek the guidance of a loving Heavenly Father. Through prayer alone does the ideal become clear; through prayer alone can she hope to be wise enough to give the help needed in human perplexities.

One quality vital to the minister's wife that had troubled me always, during the past year has become an inspiration—

humility, or teachableness. If there is another imperative for our vocation, it is teachableness. "Blessed are the meek, for they shall inherit the earth," and that means my little spot of the earth, even my small corner of opportunity. Here is a beatitude that Christ gave to his disciples; and if he gave it to his first disciples, he would also give it to the wives of the present-day disciples. Meekness is the soul of it. A trained, vibrant spirit with a willingness to be taught and to learn assures a joyous service in what is, I believe, the highest calling open to womanhood—that of the minister's wife.

Finally—and finally, sisters, not brethren this time—I repeat that prayer has all the answers. Yes, it is the soul's breath. It is the spirit's companion.

As a minister's wife, may I turn to "my" minister for the last word:

> I do not ask, O Lord,
>   A life all free from pain;
> I do not seek to be
>   In this great world of need
> Without my load of care,
>   For this I know—
> The present cross is my eternal gain
>   And he who struggling battles on
> At last shall enter in
>   And be a victor there.
>
> So, Lord, just keep me fit within
>   And give me strength to fight;
> And I will follow through the din
>   From darkness up to light.
>   —DANIEL A. POLING

VII

HER HOME

RUTH STAFFORD PEALE

ONE DAY, in the never-ending rush of busy days, as I was about to leave for another "meeting," I lifted my little daughter, then aged five, in my arms and, holding her close, her head on a level with my own, stood before a long mirror. She looked at herself and me thus reflected and excitedly said, "Look, Mommie, I am as big as you are! Now I can go to meetings too." The implication startled me, and caused me to wonder how adequately I, with my many meetings, was fulfilling the needs of my family.

The statement is frequently made that a minister's wife should be two or three people to handle and fulfill all the duties and responsibilities placed upon her. By the nature of her husband's work she has a double function; she is both a home-maker and a quasi-public figure. If she is solely domestic, she will be subject to criticism as not upholding her part in the church work. If she neglects her home in favor of duties connected with the church, the denomination, and the community, she is likely to be accused of not properly aiding her husband nor fulfilling her womanly privilege of homemaking.

When I think of a minister leaving his church or the activities in his parish at the close of the day and going home, there is just one word that comes to my mind to convey what I feel he should find as he enters his house, and that word is "haven." As he passes the threshold, some intangible spirit pervading the place should cause him to relax, should give him a sense of well-being, should make him feel that here all is well. Undoubtedly at some time during the day or, perhaps many times, circumstances have been difficult, or he has been called upon to counsel with a troubled soul, or he has been harassed by the petty differences or gossipy jealousies of members of his congregation. He needs refreshment of body, mind, and soul. He must have a place of refuge. Thus he turns homeward, longing in his whole soul for an escape, for surcease, for some place to feel God near, some haven of rest.

What he should not find is the type of wife implied in the story of the schoolboy who was assigned the writing of a brief biography of Benjamin Franklin. After much squirming in his seat and chewing of his pencil he produced the following masterpiece: "Benjamin Franklin was born in Boston. He got on a boat and went to Philadelphia. He got off the boat and bought a loaf of bread and put it under his arm and walked up the street. A woman saw him and laughed at him. He married the woman and discovered electricity." The wearied homecoming minister has had enough "electricity." He needs peace and quiet. If he likes order in the home, there should be order. If he wants to find papers, magazines, and books as he last left them in his study, he should not be continually distraught by an overbearing housekeeper. At these points a minister's wife should adjust herself to the wishes of her husband rather than impose her will upon him.

I have asked some ministers' wives to explain the great patience, the everlasting tact, the ceaseless good humor, and the untiring listening ability of their husbands. Their answer is profound and noteworthy, "They let it out at home." That is a normal and natural procedure and indicates true understanding. The words bring a picture of patient wives sitting by the hour, perhaps, listening to the outflow of whatever needs to be released from the inner soul of a man to keep him normal, happy, and convinced that the world is fundamentally good. Maybe the talk becomes heated. All the better. His soul is fired by littleness, or injustice, or sadness. As all of that flows out and into the waiting, understanding, and sympathetic ears of his wife, the soul is cleansed, flushed out as by a spring, and he is ready again to cope with the problems that repeat each day.

Here a wife must be as wise as a serpent and as harmless as a dove. If she kindles the flame which heated the talk, there is no cleansing. If she is mean, vindictive, jealous, or sensitive, she is of no help; in fact, her husband will know this and never share with her in this manner. I have known situations where the minister after his crowded day comes wearily home only to sit patiently through a rehearsal of petty jealousies that have touched his wife. For such couples my heart aches.

One of the chief though perhaps unconscious factors which create high tension in a minister is that he is never completely detached from his work. He maintains no hours. Unlike the businessman, he cannot close the door of his shop, for he is always on call. If he is not engaged in pastoral work or the duties of parish administration, his sermonic responsibility is constantly on his mind. Every effort should be made to provide him as much detachment as his profession will allow.

If his study and office are in the church, he should, so far as possible, do his studying and transact his business at that place. When he comes home, he should enjoy the privilege of going into his library to read, for the sheer enjoyment of reading, not as one who is using a tool. In his study he is a craftsman. In his home library he ought to be allowed to be a scholar or merely a reader of good books. It is true that he will make notes of material to be used, but the tools of workmanship should be scanty and the atmosphere and furnishings of the room such as will make it a place of relaxation and intellectual enjoyment. The papers, letters, memoranda, plans, diagrams, card files, telephone numbers, which comprise office paraphernalia should be kept in the office. A minister has a right to have a home that is a home and not a workshop.

Where the study and office are in the home, as is the case in many communities, they should be confined to one room, and the materials used in work and study should be kept in that room. Most assuredly the bedroom should never be cluttered with reminders of work. How can a minister peacefully sleep when on his dresser repose letters, memos, and notes not yet cared for? He should have a door he can close upon all the busy work of his world, and as it clicks shut he should have the gracious privilege of living in family life like any other man.

In the situation where the study is in the house, the wise minister's wife can see to it that in the living room novels, stories, biographies, current magazines, periodicals, and other general reading are attractively accessible, but no religious or theological books. These belong in the study, for they are part of the working tools. Imagine a grocer bringing his scales and scoops and other paraphernalia of his trade home to his parlor!

The pressure on a minister of the constant weight of his work may not be realized, but I am persuaded it has an enormous effect upon his nervous and emotional life. He needs the opportunity to divert his mind into new channels, to have momentary escape into different compartments of existence, the result of which will be the return, with new vigor and mental freshness, to the main activity of his life.

73

Financial troubles are seldom absent from the minister's household, and the situation is generally either monetary chaos or efficiency depending upon the capabilities of the minister's wife. Many extra demands are put upon the minister's family which continually strain the budget to the limit. The family must always be well dressed. The minister and his wife wish to support and be a part of community activities of an educational and cultural nature, and these cost some money. Their house must be supplied with current magazines and books in order to keep abreast of the times. The children are sent to college. Summer vacations, including as much travel as possible, are real necessities. Thus we could continue listing expenditures which in most families of average income would be considered luxuries, but which in the minister's household are part of the equipment demanded of the minister and his wife for the place of leadership they hold in the community.

What is the solution? This practical problem is faced in every clergyman's household. Some solve it with success; others are never ahead of the bills. Let us consider some suggestions.

First of all, there must be a plan. We generally call it a "budget," but a plan involves much more than a mere manipulation of figures. A plan, including a goal, as well as the charting of a course, is the first step toward financial solvency. In the plan every item of household necessity must be taken into consideration. If the total exceeds the family income, intelligent reductions on a percentage basis on some or perhaps all items, or more drastic cuts on the least necessary items must be made. The plan should be formed carefully. All members of the family should understand it and pledge co-operation. Then it should be rigorously enforced.

Food, clothing, and shelter are basic necessities. Shelter is usually provided in the form of a parsonage or manse. Food and clothing must be purchased out of a salary. Near the top on the list of necessities in a minister's household are books, and certain magazines such as religious periodicals and widely read current magazines. In most cases, I presume, we would say that a car is a necessity. However, too much strain is often placed upon the salary by too frequent changes in an automobile. Most family budgets constantly have the item "new car financing expense." Especially on smaller salaries a car should be kept longer than now is the custom. The whole motor sales industry has been built up on frequent car changes, so that a family never really owns a car, save in that vague thing called "equity." The war emergency is showing us all how long a car can last, and family budgets will profit by this lesson.

There are many other things which we have come to regard as necessities which really are not necessities. An electric washing machine, for example, is a fine thing to have, but clothes can be washed without it. It is a possession to anticipate owning. But many people persuade themselves that they must have this luxury, or some other, at once. As a result they are carrying several monthly payment plans at the same time. Little wonder is it that they never get ahead or that they sometimes fail to meet expenses. A good question to ask—and it is well to ask it incessantly, even ruthlessly—is, "Must I have this? Can I get along without it?" It is surprising what you can get along without and never miss. That is really one of the subtle secrets of living, to learn how much one can get along without.

If you decide on something you must have and want with all your heart, then it is worth working for and waiting for. Cut down somewhere just a little and save for it in a special fund. Save until you can buy it outright or at least pay the greatest part of the cost, and continue to use extra money, such as wedding fees, for that one thing until the account is closed before buying anything else. Don't get a washing machine, an electric sweeper, and a new radio at the same time. This planning and saving gives the joy of finally attaining something long sought and removes the necessity of using expensive time-payment plans. You can use your new possession with greater delight when you know that you own it, that it is paid for.

It perhaps is not very pleasant to practice this disciplinary self-control, but there is a character element in it that will not do your children any harm. They will develop for themselves the old American philosophy of frugality, thrift, and joy of ownership. Work for it, save for it, pay for it: this is good business and good character as well.

The greatest fault in most budget plans is the lack of adequate emphasis on the importance of planned saving. Experience shows that no one ever saves without planning for it. The happy thought that next year you will put something away for a rainy day never becomes a reality unless a start is made *now*. You will never save unless you determine to do so *now*. Every minister's family could save a small amount each month, regardless of how meager the income may be. It would seem that a person should save not less than five per cent of his salary in cash apart from insurance. As a practical suggestion, with your husband fix upon a reasonable and possible percentage of the family income that can be saved, and deposit this amount regularly in a savings account. For example, if the salary is $1,200 a year, or $100 per month, determine that the first act upon receiving the monthly salary will be to take $5 or $10 or whatever percentage is decided upon and set it aside in a savings account. The psychology is to say, "This salary is not $100 but

$95 a month or $90 a month, and with that we must live."

Savings once put into a savings account should not be withdrawn unless in the direst emergency. A savings account that may be easily invaded is of little value. The whole psychology of saving is disciplinary and must be self-imposed and adhered to with Spartan steadfastness. Certainly any minister's wife can help her husband to save, whether the plan be to put aside a few dollars in cash each month, buying War Bonds or building up a bank account, or to make semiannual or other payments on a reliable insurance policy. And, as mistress of the budget, she can teach her family, even the youngest, to save.

Turning from the money problem, let us look at one of the great human opportunities of a minister's wife. It is her privilege to rear her children in an unusually creative tradition. By this I mean that she may take advantage of the fact that out of ministers' homes have come traditionally successful, interesting, and worth-while men and women. Ministers' children, taken generally, have done exceedingly well, and occupy positions of influence in every walk of life.

What is there in the family life of a minister's home which, properly cultivated, has the capacity to make great people? Foremost is the pervasive influence of religion as the overall atmosphere of the home. It reveals itself, not only as the business in which the father is engaged, but in the attitudes which the children know from infancy. They are trained to accept prayer and the reading of the Bible and the singing of great hymns and personal religious work as an integral part of the daily life. These things are deeply embedded in their experience and have the effect of inducing true greatness, as is inevitably the case where men habitually live with God. They inherit faith as some children inherit money and land.

In one degree of sincerity or another it may be said of the minister's children that from the beginning "in him they live and move and have their being." It must be admitted that in some parsonage homes the foregoing is true only in small measure, but history demonstrates the remarkable power of the religious home to produce great people. Even where it is practiced imperfectly, the results obtained are superior to those brought forth from the irreligious or pagan home.

The clergyman's home is likely to be a place of intellectual influence. The minister deals with ideas. Thinking is part of his business. The children are reared under the influence of ideas that go beyond the ordinary furniture of day-by-day existence. Such children have the opportunity of knowing great books. The distinguished men of literature and history become familiar household names. Members of this household are surrounded by books, and either they learn to love them or at least they assume that books are necessary to the cultivated man. Under such an influence their minds have a tendency to expand and even to acquire the love and faculty of scholarship. Thus, whatever line of work they may later take up, they bring to it a belief in scholarship and study, all of which makes for superior efficiency.

My little boy, aged five, living in a house that is overflowing with books, surprises me repeatedly by his evidence of interest in books. He loves to handle them, to feel them, and comes to me often saying, "May I have this for my very own?" On several occasions, when I have tucked him in at night I have been amused and yet touched to see some profound work of literature lying in his nursery.

Another factor which makes for superior development in the children of the parsonage is one of the most important qualities any individual may possess. He may have every benefit including education, position, and wealth; but unless he has this quality he cannot be a great person. The quality to which I refer is insight, and particularly insight as it refers to a knowledge of human nature.

A minister deals with people, and deals with them in an intimate manner, so that he develops understanding and broad charity and forbearance—in other words, insight, or the ability to see into the motives of men. He understands why people do what they do even when they do not understand it themselves. He sees into or behind surface manifestations. His profession makes him a deep student of human personality; and if he is a good minister, he develops into a very wise man, with a mellowed and matured philosophy of people and events.

I may be presumptuous in voicing the opinion that a wise minister's wife will absorb from her husband this unusual understanding of people by reason of her patient listening to the analysis by which her husband arrives at his conclusions. But beyond this it is my thesis that the astute wife brings to this understanding the native intuitions of the feminine nature. These intuitions are potential in all women, but the peculiar domestic and public character of the position of a clergyman's wife gives the feminine intuition a unique development. Thus, in the home, the minister's wife can make to her husband certain judicious contributions to the analysis of the varied types of individuals with which he deals, helping immeasurably.

Insight is something that cannot be taught. No school can teach a course in insight because it is not communicated in that way. It grows through a process of experience and absorption. In the hearing of their children it is good practice for the minister and his wife, in a way that is kindly and free from gossip, to discuss on a high level various types of people. Over a period of years, when this is done by an understanding husband and wife, it is better than a course in psychology.

The minister's child is of course made to understand that his father's position depends upon his never repeating what he hears in the home. He early learns, therefore, that primary rudiment of the wise man, to keep his lips sealed, to listen and not to talk, to think objectively, to weigh and understand men, to analyze and evaluate, and to do all this, as far as possible, on an impersonal basis. He also learns to throw over all the mantle of charity.

Thus the parsonage youth grows to manhood ever deepening that gift called insight. In whatever occupation he enters in later years, he will have cause to give thanks for the wise and sagacious mother and father who reared him in that most subtle and common-sense institution, the American parsonage.

I never quite appreciated the true nobility of the minister's wife in the home until a recent experience clearly revealed it. I spent nearly three months on a Hollywood motion picture set with my husband, who served as technical adviser representing the Protestant churches in the filming of the first great motion picture ever made about an American clergyman, *One Foot in Heaven.*

The setting of this play is in the small towns of Iowa and Colorado during the early years of this century. The life story of the Reverend William Spence, true-to-life ministerial hero, involves a series of difficult churches and sad and dilapidated parsonages. This minister, during much of his ministerial life, received a very small salary—so small in fact and so irregular in payment that often a wedding fee actually represented manna from heaven.

HER HOME

A fine character is drawn of a man utterly devoted to his work, a great human figure, and the play is both amusing and wistful because it deals with the dear old American things and the church and home and particularly mother. The role of the parsonage mother is portrayed by Martha Scott, whose personality is one of sweetness and light. As Miss Scott frequently told me, it was her deep wish to capture the mood and with true grace portray the part of a patient, hard-working minister's wife who had little to work with in the way of money, but who made a beautiful home for her husband and children. She considered it a part of rare power, and she played it so.

The minister's wife is portrayed by Miss Scott as having a delicious sense of humor. She has several children; but perhaps her greatest child is her husband, whom she loves, admires, and understands. He inspires her and amuses her, and she knows him through and through. She is patient with his foibles, tender in his discouragements, and sturdy as the rock of Gibraltar in his hours of crisis. She is loyal unto death, saying, "Whither thou goest I will go; and where thou lodgest I will lodge: thy people shall be my people, and thy God my God," even though that means leaving a beautiful new parsonage to go back to a poor one because the latter "call" has challenged her husband.

I shall never forget the new vision I received of what a minister's wife in the home should be by watching the filming of a particularly moving scene. Everyone on the lot, from electricians and workmen to the director, was misty-eyed as he watched this scene; and that is unusual among seasoned actors of Hollywood.

The parsonage where the scene takes place is an unusually

81

bad one, having nineteen leaks. Distressed beyond words one terribly rainy day, the minister goes out on the futile quest of getting someone to do something about it. He returns home to find his faithful wife standing over the old-fashioned coal range, cooking stew for the evening meal. A new leak has opened, and the water drips down on the stove itself, where it sizzles away in a kind of futile despair.

Wearily the husband leans against the kitchen table and says, "Is that a new one?"

"Yes," replies Mother, "it just started."

Father continues, "That makes twenty leaks. It's indecent."

"I'm trying to keep it from falling in the food," says Mother. Then, with a twinkle in her eye, "But if the stew tonight is a little weaker than usual, you'll know the reason why."

She goes about her work, and Father just stands there looking at her with a rather strange look on his face. Turning, she sees him and says, "Take off your coat, Will. Why are you standing there staring at me?"

Father's voice is wistful. "Because I'm seeing you for the first time."

Mother inspects the stew. "What an absurd thing to say. You've seen me every day for twenty years."

Father continues to gaze at her. "That's just what I mean. I haven't been able to see the forest for the trees."

"Whatever you're saying, I'm sure, is very profound, Will, but you'll catch cold if you don't get out of those wet clothes."

"I'm seeing you as you are, Hope, the wife of a parson. I'm remembering the trials you've had to put up with, the series of parsonages you've had to live in and bring up your children in —each home dingier than the other. Cast-off furniture, rag rugs woven by the Ladies' Aid, pictures on the wall that the parishioners could no longer stand to have hanging on their own walls. I'm remembering your dream of having a nice home."

Mother offers him a taste of the stew, and then he goes right on. "And your work in the church—Sunday school, missionary societies, the So-and-So Club, the Committee for the Alleviation of the Plight of the Poor, a full-time job in itself. Still you've found time to manage and keep clean a house, cook and mend and scrub for a family, rear children as community models, and comfort a husband. And you've borne all this with the serenity of a Madonna."

Mother is touched. "Why, thank you, Will. There's nobody can turn a phrase as well as you can."

That day in Hollywood when this sequence was filmed and at other times during the making of the picture I noticed something deeply moving. When the actors and technicians and laboring men worked in scenes where was featured the minister's wife, a tender look came to their faces. They were seeing Mother—their own mothers—and remembering her patience, her long hours of labor and toil; they were remembering her prayers and her loving care. The soft touch of a mother's hands and a sweet face such as only she could have came once again to their thoughts. They were living it all over again; and they, whose daily work is the illusion of the screen, were gripped by a profound reality.

All good mothers are sweet and strong and inspiring, but I like to feel that the mothers of the parsonage are just a bit exceptionally so.

VIII

HER CHILDREN

NELLIE SNOKE BREWBAKER

"Poor little girls," the neighbors and friends of George MacDonald were wont to say as they thought of the five daughters of the parsonage. "It is just too bad they can have so few advantages."

The Reverend Mr. MacDonald was a Methodist preacher in London on a salary of $750 a year, and few indeed were the material advantages in that home. It was necessary for the mother to cook, clean, sew, and mend; and the girls had to assist in order to keep the domestic machinery running smoothly. But see those girls in later life. Four of them married. The first became Lady Edward Burne-Jones, wife of the great artist. The second married Sir Edward Poynter, president of the Royal Academy. The third married John Kipling, and became the mother of Rudyard Kipling. The fourth joined her life with that of a man by the name of Baldwin, and her son was Stanley Baldwin, prime minister of England. Poor little girls indeed! It was too bad they could not have had "advantages."

The facts of the story above are paralleled in the Soong family of China. The penniless mess boy who was converted in a Methodist revival in a Wilmington, North Carolina, church and became a preacher in that denomination, first in this country and later in his native China, was Charles J. Soong, head of China's most famous family. His home was an outstanding Christian home, and the three sons and the three daughters born to Charles and Katherine Soong have all attained eminence in both political and religious circles. All have been educated in America's leading universities. The youngest member of the Soong family is no less a personage than Madame Chiang Kai-shek.

The criticism is often made that ministers' children go without religion even as the shoemaker's children go without shoes. This is simply an old saying and cannot be taken at its face value. If there should be any truth in it, it is only in the rare instance, the exception that proves the rule; for statistics show the very opposite. A larger proportion of ministers' children attain distinction than children of men in any other profession. May I bring some facts to bear on this rather bold assertion? Remember that not two one-hundredths of one per cent of the people in the United States are clergymen. Now we quote from *Who's Who in America*—1924-25: "On the basis of the full returns received, it appears that 2,695 persons or 11.1 per cent in the volume for 1922-1923 had a clergyman for a father. In addition, a considerable number reported their father as 'farmer and preacher,' 'teacher and preacher,' etc."

Of fifty-one Americans in the Hall of Fame, ten were sons of clergymen. There have been three preachers' sons and seven preachers' daughters in the White House. Nine of the signers of the Declaration of Independence were sons of preachers.

Some time ago the *Philadelphia Ledger* made an investigation as to ministers' sons. The result was this paragraph:

Instead of furnishing the nation with a galaxy of scalawags, the clergy have made their sons men of distinction and no small prestige. We are told that one-twelfth of all the men whose biographies appear in *Who's Who* are sons of clergymen. England's *Dictionary of Biography* reveals an even greater preponderance of clerical forebears of noted men. Sons of clergymen are nearly double the number of sons of lawyers and physicians combined. Who in American history were the sons of preachers? Of famous writers there stands Emerson, Holmes, Lowell, Bancroft, Parkman, Sloan, Gilder, and Henry James. In politics the answer to the roll call is equally impressive. Sons of ministers include Henry Clay, President Buchanan, President Arthur, Senator Quay, Senator Beveridge, Senator Dolliver, President Wilson, and Chief Justice Hughes. Then there is the immortal Field family, embracing Cyrus W., who laid the first Atlantic cable; David Dudley, the renowned lawyer; and Stephen J., the United States Supreme Court Justice. And the equally renowned Beecher family, which includes Henry Ward Beecher and Mrs. Stowe, author of *Uncle Tom's Cabin*. The father of Agassiz was a preacher; and of Samuel F. B. Morse, inventor of the telegraph; and of Mergenthaler, inventor of the linotype machine. The list is inexhaustible, and in it blaze such names as those of Oliver Goldsmith, Linnaeus the naturalist, Jenner, the father of vaccination for smallpox, Ben Jonson, William Cowper, Sir Joshua Reynolds, Charles Spurgeon, Lyman Abbot, Joseph Addison, and President Grover Cleveland. Instead of being amiable vagabonds, the sons of clergymen come pretty close to the rank of topnotchers in every field of human progress.

The parsonages of our country furnish young men for the ministry far out of proportion to their numerical strength. In the ministers' families, one out of every fifty becomes a clergyman. From all other families, one out of every three thousand.

The minister and his wife are usually people of high ideals who put spiritual values first and whose home is spiritual in its atmosphere, purpose, and activities. The most distinctive mark of a Christian home is the personal religious life of the parents, communicated by them through the experience of their daily living. Spiritual rather than material qualities in the life of

86

parents cannot fail to be important in their influence on the children in the home. Children born and reared in a Christian home have an inheritance of inestimable value in the good name they are permitted to bear and in the splendid home training which wise Christian fathers and mothers provide. In conversation recently, a fine upstanding young soldier said very modestly when complimented on the good life he was living in spite of the temptations of his army surroundings, "My father gave me a good name, I can do no less than respect it." The influences that surround the child during his formative years will remain to color his whole later life. Truly, "as the twig is bent, the tree is inclined."

Much has been written in recent years on Christian family life, and most intelligent Christian parents give thought and concern to the providing of those things which make for the best interests of their children. Naturally the same family functions are performed in ministers' homes as in other homes. According to a bulletin of the International Council of Religious Education, some of these functions are: providing care, protection, and nurture; transmitting principal customs and ideals of the society of which the individuals are a part; providing guidance in learning to use things for the satisfaction of interests and ambitions, and in learning to give social expression to feelings and desires in relations with others; learning to live together in the home. Thus life in the family supplies nourishment for intellectual, emotional, social, and spiritual growth. The minister and his wife with patience and wisdom will seek to supply each child with this nourishment. In such a home the child is really a person and the rights of all are safe, guarded by mutual love. Dr. G. Walter Fiske says, "The home is a place to develop character, initiative, unselfishness, and ability to co-operate successfully." In the minister's home these qualities are most likely to come to their highest fruition.

In addition to spiritual advantages there are educational, cultural, and social advantages which might be mentioned. A high percentage of ministers' children go to college. The minister and his wife feel that their children must be educated, and so are ready to make whatever sacrifice is necessary. This very often entails a real hardship; but where income is limited, the young people share in the work, thus learning the value of money and also learning to use it for the essentials. This makes for self-reliance and appreciation of opportunities. It makes, too, for a spirit of family loyalty and good comradeship that is seldom experienced when college bills are paid out of an always comfortably large bank account.

The majority of preachers' children go to church colleges, and there maintain their high ideals and oftener than not find their Christian mates, who may be ministers. Although some parents think the worst that could befall their daughter would be for her to marry a minister and subject herself to the "poverty of the parsonage," nevertheless that life has compensations of which the laity has little knowledge. "I always wanted to marry a minister," said a young matron of my acquaintance who did that very thing, "and that ought to be a good testimony for being brought up in a minister's family." Only those who have passed this way can appreciate the rich and full experiences which are a part of every true minister's home.

The minister's children always have the opportunity of knowing the best people in the community. They have the privilege, too, of knowing and associating with leaders of their church and denomination, with missionaries and many other prominent persons as they come and go on their various missions. These people are most often entertained in the parson-age; their presence offers an opportunity to learn of the wider reaches of the Kingdom and opens up new interests on the part of the young people which often become the determining factor in the choice of their life work. The experiences related, the conversations at the table, even the very presence of such people all contribute to a feeling of ease and poise in meeting and associating with those whom they have been taught to respect and honor.

In the minister's home will usually be found the best in books and magazines suitable to the various ages. Pictures and music also contribute largely to the culture of the home, and advantages along these lines are given even though at a sacrifice. Ministers will always try to give their children the best in entertainment and recreation, thus meeting a need which every child has and creating a taste and desire for the best. Travel, too, has its place, and most ministers' families get about over the country even if it is just in moving from one parish to another.

Ministers' children usually form the habit of going to church. This in itself is an advantage of no small significance, for the regular church attendant is possessed of something which stands him in good stead as he faces the perplexing and difficult situations of daily living. It helps to cultivate assurance and a conviction that the church has a purpose and a mission to fulfill. As Lowell Thomas has said recently, "The church is the most basic of all our institutions and more than any other holds the key to national unity and national welfare."

Some people might lift their eyebrows in a supercilious manner if the statement were made in their presence that ministers' children have social advantages. They no doubt think at once of the things ministers' children must not do. They cannot go here, they cannot go there, they musn't do this, or they mustn't do that because they have been brought up in a parsonage. I never could see why there should be a different standard set up on that basis. To my way of thinking some things are right and others are wrong, and that is the basis on which to decide what one must or must not do. It is not fair to a child to make his father's profession his only guide of conduct. It is at this point that the wise parent leads his child to want to do right because it is right. There is grief here for the parents who are not able or willing to substitute for the questionable things something that will be enjoyable as well as satisfying to the child's social nature.

Some years ago a number of ministers' families living in the same neighborhood faced this problem and solved it to the satisfaction of parents and children alike. They formed what they called the Friday Night Club. They met in the different homes every other Friday night, choosing that night because it was most free from school and church affairs. There were children in the group from the lower grades up to and including the high school age, and each age group formed its own little circle and had games and entertainment suitable to the age. The parents also found much of common interest, and often the entire group played together. In the summer, frequent picnics and hikes were enjoyed. Autumn often found the entire crowd at the football games; winter furnished sport in coasting and skating parties, and of course the good movies were not passed by. The rules of the club were very few. The grown-ups must not "talk shop." The meeting was to be a time of recreation for everybody; and refreshments, if any, must be kept simple.

This club met a real need. It furnished recreation and relaxation, and was looked forward to with eagerness by young and old. The children are all grown and through college now, and without exception are in positions of honor in their chosen professions. The friendships formed in those wholesome social contacts have been cherished through the years by all the members of the group. The same sort of thing can be done in any community. Those parents are wise who will give themselves to guiding and sharing in the social life of their families.

Need we go further? The children of the parsonage have advantages which cannot be set forth in words, intangible somethings which are of "inestimable value," as said a young woman who grew up in a parsonage and now, married to a layman, still maintains in her home the ideals which were of such value in her upbringing. The greatest advantage of all, mentioned and left unsaid, comes from having sane, sensible, godly parents who accept in full the responsibilities which children in the home bring, and endeavor to discharge those responsibilities in such a manner as will command the love and respect of the children and fit them for the highest usefulness in society.

> Happy is the family
>   In which God is an unseen partner,
> And the religion of the home
>   Is to treat one another as God wills;
> And to seek good
>   For all families of mankind.[1]
>   —LELAND FOSTER WOOD

[1] "The Unseen Partner," from *Beatitudes for the Family*, Hearthside Press, Flushing, N. Y., p. 44. Used by permission.

IX

HER FRIENDS

MARY HANSFORD BROWN

ONE OF the most effective ways in which the minister's wife can find her place in the scheme of things is to take heed to the proverb, "A man that hath friends must show himself friendly." The value of friendship cannot be measured in this world. If the minister's wife can share with her husband in the life of the church and is sustained by the affection of the great and widespread family of the church, that will be full reward for the difficult and ofttimes insurmountable problems she meets. Many are the ways in which making friends can be of infinite value. People are lonely and need a friendly visit. Many are in trouble or sorrow and need friends. Dr. E. Stanley Jones tells of a man who said to him in a busy traffic center, "I need God, and I want you to help me find Him!" Varying customs and problems of the small church with its lean treasury, the new church with its problem of worldliness, the old church with its traditions, the large church with its far-reaching opportunities, can still be met and molded into usefulness through love and prayer coupled with a winsome friendliness.

The minister's wife's choice of friends is in large measure made with entrance to the manse, as along with her position come the friends of the parish and the associations that grow into friendship. When most people move into a new community, they are confronted with the dread of not finding their own kind and class of people. This does not often apply to the minister's wife. With her husband she is met at the train, "greeted" at the church, included in the most cultured and intellectual groups, invited into the loveliest homes. If she is lonely or unhappy it is her own fault.

There is never a dull moment for the lady of the manse, for there are always guests coming or going, or "staying over." Happily, it has always been to us a real privilege to entertain our friends. For example, there are the missionaries, home on furlough, always welcome. Not many years ago we had as our guests a missionary couple from Africa and their four children, all under seven years of age, one only a babe in arms. The other three had just recovered from infantile paralysis before leaving the mission field, and all—bless them!—had to wear braces of various kinds. On Thanksgiving morning I offered to stay with the children while the parents, who had looked forward to a Thanksgiving service in the homeland, went to church with my husband. Not having been blessed with children myself, I was in somewhat of a quandary as to how to entertain two little girls and a boy, but one need never worry about that with missionary children—at least, these proved quite resourceful. At my question of what we should do, "Why, let's have a Thanksgiving service!" all three little voices cried. So, finding an appropriate scripture passage and sitting down at the piano, I asked, "Now what shall we sing?" In trio again they answered, "Come, Ye Thankful People, Come." I read the scripture, they each offered a prayer of thanks to God, and they sang every verse of the hymn! These little children, all crippled, the oldest one permanently, had the teaching of a mother and father who manifested by their own lives of faith the blessing of prayer and praise to God no matter what the cross. I could hardly see the music through my tears, but that was the most profound Thanksgiving sermon I have ever heard.

After World War I, there were appeals for the "Near East Relief" work. One Sabbath a Persian missionary was to speak at our church, and came to us unexpectedly Thursday for the week end. My faithful servant had failed to appear that morning, with many of her household duties left undone, and while in the midst of these I was called to the hospital to my sister and a new niece. Naturally, it was with great effort that I prepared luncheon for our Persian guest; but to my utter amazement, he ate nothing but some peach preserves, which he put into his tea. We found him a much-traveled and interesting conversationalist, and Sunday his appealing messages brought a generous response from our people. Sunday night our director of young people's work was stricken suddenly ill, and it was necessary that she be brought to our home. Our Persian guest offered to sleep downstairs on the sofa—it was "better than the beds of my suffering people," he said—and he found it comfortable enough to stay for another week. But he was an appreciative guest; not a single year since has he missed sending us a Christmas card with a gracious message. Surely the "prophet's chamber," through whose doors have gone both the distinguished and the humble, has been a source of benediction to our home. People who do not open their homes to entertain the guests of the church are poorer than they think.

Outside the manse, few people realize the strain and haunting presence of sickness and sorrow there day after day, yet if in some measure we minister to the suffering we can hear the Son of Man say, "Ye did it unto me." These conditions, however, make it more imperative that we have friends; and, although it is not wise for the minister's family to show partiality, there are

94

always those in the congregation who seek the comradeship of their pastor and his wife. Second only to one's own family, who loyally stand by through the years, are these new friends we make. When we go out as "strangers and foreigners," and find a friendly church, a praying church, with people who take us into their hearts and homes, our love goes out to them in gratitude. We have become "fellow citizens with the saints," and again the manse becomes our home.

Always ready to befriend the poor and lowly, the minister and his wife must not forget that the "underprivileged," while more in need of material things, are no more in need of the Gospel than the privileged, or as someone has said, the "over-privileged." This may bring some criticism from lack of under-standing, but what a wonderful faith we have seen manifested by those with material blessings who know that God can provide what money and influence cannot buy. They need the church and the church needs them, not nearly so much for their money as for their contributions of time and consecration of talent. Many large gifts to foreign missions have been made through the friendship of the minister's family, but harm may have been done when the motive of so-called friendship has been "gifts." Christ's command was "Go ye and teach," "preach," "witness" for him; and if we obey his commission, will he not provide for the maintenance of his work? However, the home church must support all causes of the church; and so missions at home and abroad, education of youth for the ministry, care of aged ministers, Sunday school extension, all must have the interest of the ministers. Friends can be raised up for these causes by forceful presentation of the needs and tactful enlistment of members of the church and by the invaluable co-operation of the women's auxiliaries.

As in the Apostle Paul's day, Christians have "gifts differing." There are those among the wives of ministers who have God-given talents valuable to the work. These govern to some extent the friendships and social activities. For example, if the minister's wife is gifted and educated musically, the choir and musical circles can be her main lines of communication with friends. This can be a contribution to the spiritual development of the church, an addition to the cultural growth of a community, an approach to indifferent people, a help to her husband, and a source of joy and recreation to her. I say it can be; but one display of temperament may cause heartache and, in modern parlance, "headache" for many.

The gift of executive ability can also be an asset if not used too freely on the poor husband. A small church needing, and wanting, leadership in the work of the women is most fortunate to have a minister's wife who can lead the people in their projects. If hers is a consecrated leadership, her influence for good will be valuable to the church.

There is also the gift of entertaining, and in the home of a minister the social graces are an acceptable gift. Social relationships abroad are valuable, but it is also important to bring the congregation into the manse. While living in Oxford, England, I was impressed with the delightful informality of the "four o'clock tea." Although a regular meal in the household, it is shared with the guests as if they belonged there. The thin slices of buttered bread, the pound cake, the marmalade and, of most importance, the tea, are there for the taking, the hostess pouring her own tea. This, after a fashion, put into use on an "at home" day or an occasion for church groups has been found a pleasing change from the formal tea. People who love to entertain can find a way to repay courtesies in some gracious manner. The most effective way we have found is our traditional "Open House" or "Christmas Party" for the congregation. While the house radiates its welcome through the glow of Christmas candles and the sound of Christmas carols, we love to open wide the door to those who, with us, want to "rest beside the weary road, and hear the angels sing."

Most needed, and perhaps most neglected, of all Christian friendship is that among young people, and the social life of the Church is important in reaching them if attractively sponsored. As we look through the gathering shadows of our beloved country today, it is the youth who are to make the greatest sacrifices and play the important roles. When traveling anywhere one sees soldiers and sailors looking wistfully from train windows, lying on hard station benches, and too often drinking in club cars of the trains. Of all people who need faith, the youth of our land come first. Having had two young nephews in our home during their college days, we know that with true patriotism and courage undaunted the young men will meet their call to service; but shall we send them forth to battle without the "whole armor of God"? From work already done among young people the occupants of the manse have seen the best results of their efforts. Those dear friends they have followed with interest and prayer are many of them outstanding as ministers and missionaries, or as secular leaders. It is a joyous privilege to have any part in molding a good life, but more joyous still when it is surrendered to the work of the Master; and this is the hope of our church, yea, even our country, for tomorrow!

Children in the home limit, of course, its social activities, but perhaps the gift of some is that of being a mother to the children of the manse. We know a brilliant woman who was a prac-

ticing physician before her marriage to a minister, and she
continued practicing until the twins came to their house. Now
she has given up all, except to keep up in her reading, to home
and church. Good mothers are needed in our day; in fact, we
sometimes conclude there are too few. The superintendent of
one of our large orphanages on a visit to our church talked
affectionately of his orphan children and what the school was
teaching them. He said, "They know how to play; they study
the Bible and pray; they are happy!" I wonder if many
privileged children in their own homes have that kind of training for life—and eternity. Some of the wives of the manse may
be handicapped in church work and friendships by illness,
invalidism. Then surely, they need to have the understanding
and prayers of the congregation, and I hope they always do.

Of these "gifts differing," the Scriptures instruct us to "covet
earnestly the best gifts." One sure way to find the best gifts
as ministers' wives is to start early to read and study, to love
and live, the Word of God. Some are fervent in prayer; some
have a gift of teaching. Fortified by a saving faith their service
is effectual. Other graces to covet earnestly are humility and
consecration, two of the greatest virtues. These are some of the
spiritual gifts by which we cannot but find the best way of life.
As Dr. S. D. Gordon says, "Christ has arranged for us a personally conducted tour" by sending the Holy Spirit, who, Christ
said, "shall teach you all things, and bring to your remembrance
whatsoever I have said unto you." Through him, the friends
you make, the lives you touch, will be better for your having
lived and you'll find at the end of the day of life "the souls of
the friends you've made."

X

HER APPEARANCE

LILIE BENBOW SCHERER

DURING THOSE days when the new thrill of a diamond ring on the fourth finger found my left hand always in full view, I came upon a friend who had heard the "news." With her sympathetic arm on my proud shoulder, she hailed the years ahead: "Well, my dear, when I first heard you were to marry a clergyman it seemed incredible to me, but since then I realize someone *must* marry them!"

When I was assigned this chapter on the minister's wife and her personal appearance, I felt it was the last phase of the subject I would have chosen. But there again, someone *must* do it; for personal appearance is, of course, an important aspect of that personality. Emily Post might have been asked to write on "What the Well-dressed Woman of the Manse Will Wear," or Dale Carnegie could have told us "How to Dress Well and Win New Members." But here a clergyman's wife herself has looked into her mirror, filled with ideas, plus perhaps a better understanding of the problems involved in improving that inescapable reflection.

When such a particular model realizes that, alas, she is not that fortunate lily of the field and must consider wherewithal shall she be clothed, she must at once face that sternest adviser of all, the budget! What is the average budget of the average parsonage?

Someone recently wrote an article under the caption "Wanted:

Rich Wives for Our Ministers" which created quite a sensation. Obviously the writer was keenly aware of the difficulty which the by-and-large of the clergy have in making reasonable provision for the needs of their families. From the most recent statistics available it would seem that the average income of the parson is from $1,200 to $1,500 a year. It is estimated that only one per cent receive $3,600 or more. This modest salary comes often at the end of seven to eight years of study and preparation, for which many have had to incur a certain indebtedness as a kind of mortgage on the future.

I believe there is no family unit which accomplishes more with its monthly check than does the average minister's family. It might be said that the family lives out its life on a stage, for there is always somebody looking on—persons or groups often sympathetic and understanding, sometimes critical and unfeeling. Not the personal appearance of the minister's wife only, but of each member of the family—and there usually *is* a family —is to be considered. The home they make is expected to be in good taste and attractive. Most of the children from the parsonage manage somehow to achieve an education, in which perhaps they are helped by scholarships, by part-time work, and sometimes by friends.

We must also remember that both the minister and his wife realize that the time will come for them to retire. In this the congregation frequently concurs! How much have they been able to save, and what old-age security has been planned for them? In most denominations woefully little!

One must have all these things in mind when one comes to discuss such a subject as mine. The personal appearance of every man or woman is important, but especially is this true of the individual whose life and work keep him always in close

100

contact with many people among whom he must normally assume a degree of general leadership. We all realize what an important part one's appearance plays in attracting people, repelling them, or just leaving them indifferent.

The first thing which the phrase "personal appearance" suggests is clothes, although this is only a part of the figure we cut. There are hair, hands, voice, and manner—such important parts of the whole, and often so sadly neglected! We will consider each; but because clothes come first to our mind, let us start with them. So let us take the "clothesline" in the budget, add to it all the ingenuity we have, plus the time we can spare, and what we have observed, and answer the age-old question, *What to wear?*

The minister's wife must be dollar-minded with regard to clothes. The only problem for one whose pocketbook is well filled is to find a reliable shop and coutourier, and then not to allow too great a contrast between her wardrobe and that of her co-workers in the congregation. Indeed, it has been my experience that most congregations are proud of the attractive appearance of their minister and his family. Never have I heard them spoken of as being too well dressed. There is something touching and beautifully generous about this; for very often, thanks to ingenuity, the minister's family is better clothed than many others in the congregation. The daughter of a clergyman recently wrote this to me: "For my sake, tell ministers' wives not to look like frumps. It is so unnecessary and uncalled for. Parishioners are always proud of a well-dressed lady in the parsonage, and don't hold tasteful dress as inconsistant with holiness. After all, don't all of us think of angels as beautiful creatures?" Where the minister's wife is loved for herself first, there is great leniency—sometimes a spirit almost too kindly for her good. I hesitate to admit this, for who does not love to be spoiled?

As I have said, when one can try on clothes without first asking the price, the problem is very much simplified. It is not particularly to anyone's credit to be well dressed when she can afford a shop which provides at once good materials, good taste, and an expert saleswoman who practically makes up her mind for her. Most of us who are busy people would be only too willing to give the shop the credit if we could be spared the time, energy, and painstaking planning which purchasing takes when one can have only a few clothes for many occasions. But here we share a common experience with each other and with the large majority of women in our congregations. This is one of the reasons why we are mutually appreciative of each other's good results, understanding very well the problems surmounted.

The understanding is increased when one has served and lived with the same congregation for many years, and is comfortably at home among most of them. Last fall I unearthed a gray coat from the mothballs for the fifth year. It was a much better coat than I had known when I bought it, and simply wouldn't wear out. My elder daughter came upon me eagerly searching for worn places to find a legitimate excuse for retiring it from active service. "Well," said she, "if it's that good, you could probably dye it your favorite shade of dark brown, and make it seem like a new coat." So it does; and when several of my friends in the congregation recognized the transformation and appreciatively exclaimed, "A very good idea! And even more becoming than before!" I purred under its fur collar!

To be able to make much out of little is in itself a fascinating adventure, and a very important item in the art of living. To have to think wisely and well, to plan carefully, is a discipline for which we are not always easily grateful; but at the end of that road lies deep satisfaction, and a glow on the horizon. This is perhaps a platitude, but we do well to remember it: the struggle behind any achievement is three quarters of the fun and satisfaction. One who knows recently wrote me, "All my life I've been most intimate with pastors' wives who have dressed themselves and their families on an income of less than $1,800 a year; and if the wife can catch the spirit of the game, it's really a lot of fun!" There is no occasion here for self-pity. The very necessity for careful choice sharpens not only our wits but our sense of values. A very uncommon sense!

Accepting our limitations, what are the things we must remember? First, this, that we can all afford neatness, that cardinal virtue, especially in women. It is of paramount importance—neatness literally from head to foot. No matter what the budget allows, this we can and must manage. It costs not money, but a moderate amount of time and energy; and it is a gilt-edged investment. The temptation to be a little slipshod where there are many appointments and meetings close together is very human; nevertheless, people find it also inexcusable. More than that, we do not enjoy even ourselves when we are unkempt. Somehow it makes us feel and act below par and less than our best selves. "Take time to be holy," and take time to be neat! Having little time is no excuse for little holes and little spots.

Before choosing what you will wear, study your own physical assets and liabilities. Cater to the former, and make all your substractions from the latter. Nothing is more rash than to imitate a style or buy a certain garment because "I saw this on Mrs. Smith, and it was so becoming to her!" Never be a slave to any style of headdress, or any other dress, because most

103

people in the congregation or in Hollywood are affecting it! The only valid reason for anything in your wardrobe is that it is becoming to you, and so enhances your personal appearance. Why millions of women, not two of whom look alike—there are very few identical twins!—should dress alike and standardize their hair, lips, ears, nails, feet, and body is one of the interesting phenomena of our time; and the ludicrous and almost pathetic results are only too apparent.

Make-up must always be carefully studied before being generally practiced. In a somewhat desperate and last effort to improve me, my friends urged me to try some lipstick—oh, ever so little. Whereupon we retired and carried through the experiment, with little and much. The vote was instant and unanimous that even a trace made me look as if I were bound for Venice in search of the handsomest gondolier on the Grand Canal! Nevertheless, I still contend against a certain member of my family that the well-tempered use of some forms of make-up does improve certain people, though perhaps it is true that mascara, this side of the footlights, casts a questionable shadow over the beauty of any face! For all who go to extremes I can think only of the Hollywood caption: "Any resemblance to any living person is purely coincidental!"

A very few women can wear extreme styles becomingly. The round, large moon face, encircled by an even larger, rounder, off-the-face halo hat; the raging lips and nails, usually with the first glow rubbed off, leaving a decayed effect; the too-short skirt, atop the less fortunate legs; the ensemble which looks like a boxing match of clashing colors; the massive earrings which seem to be in need of a reducing diet; the half-dozen new, cheap bracelets which have taken precedence over the two that are older and better—how many naturally attractive women have ruined their personal appearance with such devices! I suppose in many instances this common mistake is the result of a simple desire to make oneself more interesting, to break over a little from the long and irksome habit of being conservative! Unfortunately, this extremism is not an adequate short cut to that most elusive goal, attractiveness in women. Our "public" tires of extremes very quickly. Far wiser is she who is content with that becoming simplicity which lends itself so readily to attractive embellishment. The variety of things one can do to adorn a costume with a tasteful change of accessories offers a wide and interesting field for experiment. And there is always a certain freshness and satisfaction about an outfit into which has gone some ingenuity.

It is not enough to find a dress that is definitely becoming. Before you smilingly tell the clerk, in the first proud moment of possession, to wrap it up, stop to think what you have that will blend with it—hats, coats, shoes, gloves, purses, or jewelry. Choose a few, a very few colors, which you wear best, and buy only those things which will contribute to an attractive ensemble. A becoming brown hat, a becoming red dress, and a most becoming black coat and shoes will not make a becoming ensemble. Failing to take this total effect into consideration is one of the more prevalent mistakes made by the woman on the limited budget. There is a good reason why black has been the popular stand-by for so many seasons: it not only flatters the figure but lends itself complacently to individual treatment. With what is called "the simple foundation black dress" one easily and for little money has the equivalent of three or four dresses. This is part of the secret of that feeling which so many women share of being well dressed in black.

The psychological effect of our own satisfaction with the

results gives us that much-needed sense of self-confidence. For if the truth were known, most of us are painfully aware of our inadequacies in all the fields and among the many people we serve. Where the same men and women have to see us so often, it is comfortable to believe that, though they may well get tired of listening to us, they at least don't get tired of looking at us! Better, then, to possess a few costumes that have character, than double the number cheap and nondescript!

There is another phase of this subject which must be mentioned in any discussion that aims to cover the ground even superficially. Very few of us have not had relatives and friends who were as much interested in our personal appearance as we are. From time to time they have undertaken to have a hand in remedying it. Others may "dress us down"; they will dress us up! Surely now and then the gifts they send us are obviously things we could not ourselves afford; but as long as they do not violate the laws of good taste I see no reason for feeling hesitant about using and enjoying them. Naturally, this experience is not confined to the wives of ministers, and yet for them it does constitute something of a special problem. When there are so many who know fairly well what means we have, it is decidedly uncomfortable that we should even appear to be "wasting our substance" on nonessentials. In such cases we can only hope for that understanding on the part of the congregation which will attribute our good fortune to its proper and generous source. And it is difficult to conceive why we ourselves should be so reticent about mentioning it. There is a deal of false pride in such matters with which we as well as others would do well to dispense.

Any number of us could cite instances in point. I am reminded of two in my own life which came at the very height of the recent depression, when any new adornment was doubly noticeable. Both of them I have deliberately chosen to mention because they fall outside the category of those congregational thoughtfulnesses which are beyond reckoning altogether. One of them was my acquisition of a fur coat, quite manifestly beyond my means. When the expected comments were made, it seemed to me the most natural thing in the world to say, "Yes; isn't it lovely? A friend of mine sent it to me; and I'm as happy about it as a child!" I am certain that no simple, restrained, and proprietary response of, "I'm very glad you like it," would have been a genuine expression of my feeling. The other instance took place over a luncheon table. Without any preliminaries, my dearest of schoolmates took off her little-finger ring set in small pearls and diamonds and said, "My dear, I was wearing this ring when we met, twenty-six years ago, and I want you to have it." If I had been able to go down to Cartier's and buy that ring, it never would have meant what it means to me, with the genuine sentiment behind it wrapped in the beauty of it. I wear it, and it encourages and heartens me, standing as it does for so much of the best I have known in those twenty-six years. I must believe that anyone seeing it will understand that I didn't in a weak moment deposit the total loose offering for fifty-two Sundays on the counter of Tiffany and Company! The thing that none of us, nor any other person, would appreciate would be a gift sent out of pity or a mistaken sense of duty. But what people do because they are sincerely fond of us can bring us nothing but intense pleasure. So do we hope in turn that our expressions of affection will be received. To disavow that pleasure would be hypocrisy.

So too in connection with the "good buys" we are sometimes fortunate enough to make. In a group of women someone will say to you, "Oh, that's such a good-looking outfit!" Why not respond immediately, "I'm so glad you think so. I came on it in the budget shop for $5.98 and hoped it was a find!" Another will frequently nudge you and whisper, "Don't tell that. It looks like a much better dress! I thought it cost at least twenty-five!" To me the latter attitude is neither sincere nor wholesome. The credit lies not in paying so much, but in paying so little and looking so well! Yet I must here interpolate this proviso: that no minister's wife would be willing to dress at the expense of women and girls who are forced to spend dreary lives at the sewing machine or with the needle for ten cents an hour. Any intelligent woman can find out the conditions under which her "bargain" dresses were made. The Consumer's League will be glad to give her such information.

Again and again in this chapter reference has been made to "good taste." How can we guard against the pitfall of thinking we have it when others know we have not? Our parishes are often not within reach of the relatives who would so gladly advise us. But surely in every congregation or community there is some person who is universally considered well groomed, and who would be helpful and understanding in this matter. Someone has said, "If you want to make a friend ask a favor." People like to be needed. Should you ever be uncertain about your own choice, ask another's opinion. Each of us is human, and like everybody else thrives on encouragement and warmth. It is said that the dying Goethe called for "Light! More light!" To which someone has answered, "It is not more light we need. It's more warmth."

By nothing that has been said herein is it implied that in a group of women the minister's wife should easily be singled out because of her appearance. The greeting, "I knew you were the minister's wife the moment I laid eyes on you," is a doubtful compliment. One can justly be proud of being a minister's wife, but to be so obviously marked may or may not be a cause for self-gratification; it's important to find out which! Yet it would be pathetic and even tragic if out of full and varied lives we should emerge thinking, acting, and even looking like everybody else. It has always seemed to me that we should inevitably develop a richer individuality than most women. Such a varied experience as ours—touching as it does vicariously if in no other way the heights and depths of human life—should express itself inwardly as well as outwardly.

Of course no matter how devastating the costume, its effect is almost completely nullified by a careless and unattractive posture. There is a kind of carriage which the Christian faith itself should provide, with its deep convictions and its undaunted aspirations. The human body is not a rack for hats and clothes; it is a temple. To realize that is to stand erect and lift the head and square the shoulders; and at the same time to add that spark without which all our labor to look our best is in vain. It is ours to lead, with the dignity of those to whom Jesus has said, "Henceforth I call you not servants, but friends."

So far we have been considering the minister's wife as a member of society in a public outside her home. But each of us has a public inside the home! All that has been said of the former applies to the latter as well. Perhaps the peril of familiarity in the inner circle should be mentioned in this chapter. It is true that familiarity can breed "content" as well as "contempt"; but we know each other in our home for what we really are, and, amid the many responsibilities which occupy our time and energy, we allow each other on occasion the luxury of carelessness. The tempting comfort of the kimona, the reliable but soiled gingham apron, the hair in prefactory curlers—there are times and places for these mothers' helpers, but they should remain mere acquaintances and never be allowed the intimacy of long-continued friendship. Not only do we constantly set an example for each other, but the whole tone of family life is lifted or lowered by such casual habits. Cleanliness is next to godliness, and neatness is its frame! We honor one another in the graciousness of our presence.

But clothes do not make the woman any more than they make the man; and woe to her who lays too much store by them. A pleasing, soft voice and an engaging manner are within the reach of us all, and what priceless possessions they are! As to the former, if you have ever done any singing at all it has been said to you again and again, "Oh I'd give anything to be able to sing!" So indeed would I! I am comforted only when I remember that comparatively few people sing well enough to give pleasure to others. Singing is a very difficult and exacting art, and there are not many who attain to any mastery of it. But the speaking voice all of us use constantly, everywhere, with everybody; and it has always been a puzzle to me that so few people take any intelligent interest in it. We have all been subject to that mild form of torture which whining, rasping, high-pitched voices inflict; and we have known the comfort and blessing of those that are well-modulated and warm. The one sets everybody's nerves on edge; the other is at least like music in that it soothes even the savage breast.

By the soft voice, let it be understood, is not meant the voice which cannot be heard without straining every drum and sinew! To us who have been present at gatherings both small and large, nothing is more tantalizing or exhausting than the "still small voice" which conveys nothing at all to the listener, and is a definite liability to an otherwise gracious and effective presence. A moderate amount of tone and good diction are all that is required in order to be audible when playing or praying. How many meetings have been ruined by this lack in a leader who is on other counts all that one could wish! There is very little use in speaking at all when what is said is not said to be heard. If the volume of sound issuing from the lips of many a chairman is all that is available for use, I cannot understand how the family of that person ever gets together for breakfast, dinner, or supper. A voice can be pleasing and audible at the same time; if it is not both, it is a God-given talent which has been buried not in a napkin but in a chest!

As vital as a pleasing voice to the total presence is a gracious manner. While it is the outward and visible sign of an inward and spiritual grace, one can nevertheless consciously improve it. The manner of one's approach to persons and problems often determines the issue; the improvement of that manner calls for discipline. There is not one of us who feels gracious all the time and under all conditions, not even in her own family. Yet certainly none has license to express what one feels regardless of others. To do so would be utterly selfish, not only in one's family life but in every circle where one has to live and work with people. The unthinking will advise that one go to one's room and shut the door when anxiety or weariness makes it difficult to associate with others; but to appear just when she feels fit or chooses is not the lot of the minister's wife. At such times we must consciously discipline ourselves and apply a special kind of "make-up." Stand in front of your mirror; see that every furrow in the brow is removed, and that the corners of the mouth are upward bound—standing not at twenty minutes past eight, but at ten minutes of two! If this sounds childish, try it. In the family circle as well as in the congregation, and even when you are alone, it is a practice which has a singular ministry. The anxious, harassed, unpleasant expression wears our own selves out as well as others, and surely belies our creed. So, too, is it with our husbands, and indeed with all who call themselves Christian. To be singled out not so much for a beautiful as for an artless and radiant face is to be well marked; and for it the unnatural, vacant, and professional grin is never a substitute.

Finally, it goes almost without saying that the very foundation of a gracious personality is a genuine and passionate interest in people; and in those especially who are in a peculiar way our "good companions" in a distinctly Christian fellowship. To the minister's wife who has a passion for people, in sickness and in health, rich or poor, a kindly bearing should be as natural as breathing; and there is nothing which so colors her whole appearance. There are many who find others a nuisance, and are not only uninterested but frankly impatient. To them my word would be, "Consider well before you marry a minister. Least of all can a minister's wife afford such attitudes."

Surely, when all is said and done, what we seem to others is determined more by what goes on inside of us from day to day and from year to year than by anything else. The fact is at once a comfort and a challenge to those of us who cannot afford the embellishments which money can buy, and which we often are misled to believe essential. It is from an invisible treasure house that radiance is drawn, with all the joyousness of spirit which so often ennobles the plainest face and renders it "becoming." This is ultimately what dresses us up! It is this above all else that makes both men and women more even than merely good to look at!

XI

HER AVOCATION

JEAN BEAVEN ABERNETHY

IT WOULD be irrelevant, in view of the title of this book, to indulge at any length in a discussion of whether a married woman can successfully combine marriage and a career. Not that there is a dearth of things to say—and on both sides—but, as a matter of fact, the average minister's wife is not confronted with any such sophisticated alternative as marriage versus marriage *and* career. Public opinion has her functions fairly well defined and also, sad to relate, the patterns by which she must meet those functions.

Nevertheless, while it is the unusual minister's wife who faces the complex decision of combining a career with her marriage, her essential problem ought to be the problem of us all, irrespective of our vocational ambitions—namely, whether or not we propose to preserve and develop our individuality. Are we going to express ourselves within the accepted areas of wifehood, motherhood, and church responsibility *as we see fit,* and are we going to develop *other* areas for self-expression besides the above trio? Or are we going to fit into grooves already made and thereby take the line of least resistance? These are questions every minister's wife has to answer, and even refusing to recognize them is an answer in itself.

The question takes on flesh and bones if we personalize it. Let's take a hypothetical example. Mrs. G is not only the wife of the minister of the second largest Methodist church in town and the proud mother of three healthy and boisterous young-sters; she is also a musician of no mean ability, with extensive training and graduate degrees to her credit. Although Mrs. G hasn't entered the "life begins at ———" decade, nevertheless she is no longer strictly young, and she feels that, with the passing of every year, she is getting more and more out of practice on the piano. Now that her children are past the full-time demands of the preschool period, she's been toying with the idea of "doing something" with her music. What would you advise Mrs. G?

We will make our respective answers—in fact, we *are* making them every day—in terms of the way we are living our own lives; and it would not be unfair to say that the values we use in giving judgment depend pretty largely upon our own train-ing and background. There is little question that the older generation of ministers' wives would counsel Mrs. G something like this: "Let your music be a form of relaxation to you when you're tired or depressed. Have fun with it in your family life, teaching your children to appreciate good music and using your talent to bind your family group together in its recreational and cultural activities. And make yourself an asset to your husband by being willing to play the piano on the varied and many occasions in church life when good musicianship is so essential. Make music your unique contribution to family and church life, and therein you will find true and complete self-expression."

It is a good answer and not without its points. But increas-ingly, and for younger women, it lacks convincingness. Mrs. G wants to join the Friday Morning Musicale—the city's ex-clusive club for performing musicians—and with a little practice she could make the grade. There she would meet experts who talk the latest developments in her field; there she would have to compete with performers whose criticisms would perfect her own style; there she would not be "the pastor's wife" or "Johnny G's mother," but Mrs. G, whose rendering of Debussy makes her someone to reckon with in her own right.

Mrs. G has also toyed with the idea of teaching piano lessons. She was an excellent teacher with a good income when she married Mr. G. She reasons, rather surreptitiously—because she's not sure just what Mr. G will think of it, and because she *is* sure what the Woman's Society will think of it!—"If I could teach three mornings a week while the children are at school, I could make enough to hire someone to do the heavy housework, and then I could use the other two mornings to practice myself."

Poor Mrs. G! She's in for trouble. If she accepts the first answer and gains social approval, she has conflict within herself to reckon with, and society has suffered a certain amount of waste in her specialized training. If, on the other hand, she decides to branch out on her own either by participating actively in a secular group or by earning a regular income, she must be prepared to hear criticism—by those who feel they have the right to criticize since they employ her husband—that she is neglecting her home and church and that she is a selfish and ambitious woman.

If, however, she can take these barbed, and for the most part unjustified, criticisms in her stride, there is much to be said for Mrs. G's making the latter choice and "doing something" with her music outside, as well as within, the provinces of home and church life. It would mean, of course, some taking stock of how she now uses her time, some pruning, and some deciding on what functions could be abandoned without jeopardizing other values. For instance, she might decide that part of the housekeeping, or overly long telephone conversations, or certain aspects of church activity in which she engages merely in an ex-officio capacity could be given up, thereby allowing her the time to profess music rather seriously.

After Mrs. G has taken the initial step of getting her values straight and budgeting her time accordingly, what now can be said for her doing what she wants to do with her music? In the first place, it may be said, even though many in her husband's congregation will think otherwise, that ultimately her family will be the richer for it. She is not the mother who attends countless meetings, passively accepting the efforts of others, nor the mother who kills time by flitting from one tea to another only to return home at the end of the day in the same mental vacuum and in the same physically flabby condition as when she left. Nor is she the mother and wife who sits at home all day waiting for the return of her wayfarers, vicariously living their experiences with them, but gradually losing them as they mature beyond her. She is instead a sharer of accomplishments and failures made out in the world her husband and children know. She participates, competes, concentrates, has to keep intellecutally alert and physically trim in the same world where report cards and pay envelopes make her family toe the mark.

And, we must repeat, the cost of her being a *contributing* member in her household need not be too high. She can still be the integrating factor in family life and play the role we uniquely associate with "mother." Mrs. G, for example, could be in the musicale and teach two mornings a week and, having effective domestic help which she could then afford, still be fresh for her children when they come romping in from school and her husband when he comes home at night; and she could still perform a carefully selected number of church obligations with thoroughness. She has simply substituted Beethoven for dishwashing and gossip; and, given Mrs. G's ability and training, it is a socially useful substitution.

In the second place, Mrs. G is making an indirect, but none the less real, contribution to the church by participation in a secular organization. In far too many cases the church draws only those women who have no other social outlet; and in far too many instances the cultural and secular organizations in a community, ranging from the League of Women Voters and the A.A.U.W. to the more strictly professional groups, attract people who hardly know a church exists and who, if they are pressed, think of it only in stereotypes, lumping all church people together as uninteresting, unsophisticated, old-fashioned. The minister's wife in her strategic position could, by mere attendance upon some of these secular groups, begin to break down this barrier. Not that she goes forth to evangelize. Merely that, as she wins her way, someone might turn around some time and say, "I didn't know ministers' wives came as charming as that. I wonder what her husband is like. Maybe I'll go to hear him next Sunday."

But it is about time for some minister's wife to interrupt with, "This is all very well if you're talented, but I'm not. I can't play three notes on the piano; I can't carry a tune; I can't write poetry or paint a canvas; and I can't get up and give a speech if my life depends on it. In fact, I can't do anything that remotely sounds like a career, and besides I'm perfectly content to be 'the pastor's wife' and 'Johnny's mother.'"

There is no question that for some ministers' wives the prospects of becoming influential outside the home and the

117

local church has no appeal at all, either because they lack the specialized training which spurs them on, or because their health or their own inclinations make the two areas of activity quite sufficient. And no one would insist that such women strain to follow Mrs. G and deliberately cultivate "extracurricular activities" when they haven't the least desire to do so. But there is value in insisting that, within the areas most congenial to them, they too perfect themselves at some point and make their contributions unique to them.

After all, it matters not so much what one does as that in the doing of it one shall satisfy the creative urge and the desire for recognition which sociologists insist are basic in humankind. Making excellent pastry and sharing one's culinary talents with appreciative and needy neighbors; constructing a daring and stunning centerpiece out of cardboard, weeds, and melted-up old candles so that in spite of a limited budget one's table reflects ingenuity and taste; or sewing one's fourteen-year-old's first party dress in such a way that she does not think it "homemade-y" and that others rave over it—such things take time, demand effort and ability, and give as satisfying a sense of accomplishment to some women as presenting a Beethoven concerto does for others.

What we have been saying in this chapter ultimately goes back to one's definition of personality and one's philosophy of marriage. It was Kahlil Gibran's Prophet who advised Almitra, when she asked him about marriage, "The pillars of the temple stand apart, and the oak tree and the cypress grow not in each other's shadow." Too many of us women make the mistake of confusing marriage with self-negation, rationalizing our own inability and our own laziness by becoming superabsorbed in our husbands and children and living our lives through them. But true love is not the merging of personalities which can but result in the inner impoverishment of all concerned. It is more like the figure Mrs. Miniver gives us when she likens a happy marriage to a pair of intersecting circles—not on top of each other, as there would be no private resources left on either side to enrich the life that is shared; but each circle crossing the other so that the two outer crescents are as big as the section in the middle. Individuality is a precious gift and too inherent in the social scheme to be sacrificed on any altar. True love does not demand this sacrifice.

From the point of view of personality and leadership, to say nothing of successful marriage, "the pillars of the temple stand apart." Regardless of what particular temples we are building, they will endure only if each one of us does her share in supporting them, rising to the full stature the Great Architect intended for us.

XII

HER SPECIAL INTERESTS

MAE TALMAGE PRUDEN

EVERY MINISTER's wife should be an authority in some field of interest or activity, if only that she may thus become more interesting to herself, her family, and her friends. In spite of the myriad calls upon her time, her thoughts, and her efforts, she may discover that her life becomes rather drab and uninteresting at times if she permits herself to be used up in routine activities. Unless there is something of special interest to add variety and spice to life—to keep it alive and glowing when it tends to pall—the ordinary round of events may at times prove to be very monotonous. A woman who possesses an unusual interest in something is never one who has to be entertained and amused in order to be happy. She has within herself those inner resources which make for happiness at its best—happiness that is based upon interesting and rewarding experiences.

All the benefits of finding such an enthusiasm are not hers alone. The husband of such a wife will discover that his own life is made increasingly interesting by the activity that has proved to be so fascinating to her. The minister's life frequently tends to become humdrum, and a wholesome diversion is created for him when his wife can bring something new and fresh into their common experience. If she does nothing more spectacular than become really outstanding in the art of running her home or of making friends, she can contribute much to her husband's happiness. In the pursuit of her special interest it is altogether likely that she will make contacts that will prove beneficial to her husband, as well as to herself. These contacts frequently open doors of opportunity which otherwise might remain closed, and friendships develop that make of life an entirely new thing.

If there are children in the family, no special emphasis on the subject is needed to show what benefit they might derive from an environment that is enriched by the presence of a mother especially gifted in some field. A child who has been lovingly and sympathetically trained from babyhood to use his mind, to develop any artistic leaning he may have, and to use his hands has indeed a great deal in his favor if the one who guides him in these endeavors is his mother. For who can know her child better? A word spoken at the right moment, encouragement when it is most needed, surely can be better supplied by no other person. A mother's interest alone in some special subject can greatly influence the plastic minds of her children, for much is absorbed unconsciously by them from her. Her contribution to their home life is therefore the more valuable.

Moreover, a woman who has something special to bring to the lives of her friends is fortunate. To mean the most to them she should be interested in everything in general and in some one thing in particular; for, to be universally interesting, one must be universally interested. Think of some of the most charming friends you have. Why does your mind naturally turn to some and not to others? What is there about certain ones that makes you think of them rather than of others you know?

I am thinking of a certain minister's wife whose chief charm to me is her gift for conversation. She has, of course, an unfailing interest in many things that adds richness and depth to anything she says; and, through the years, she has developed spiritually and mentally to such an extent that although she is unaware of it, her face is lovely to watch as she talks. Her contribution to a conversation is so charged with sincerity that one can never fail to be impressed, and with no pretense or sham she carries others along with her. She can be serious but is never prim, or she can be gay and you laugh uproariously. She indeed possesses a gift that causes her to be sought after by all her friends. For she is the sort of person about whom people invariably say without being asked, "Isn't she nice?"

Since we are concerned here with the minister's wife particularly, we naturally would not omit one of the most important phases of her life—namely, her contribution to her church. It goes without saying that she may be of more value if only she can bring to her church relationship something a little out of the ordinary. I know of a young minister's wife who is quite in demand among groups in various churches because of her ability to make interesting chalk talks. She draws beautifully, among other things, and is naturally valuable in this way. Being quite attractive personally and possessing marked ability, she is indeed an asset to her church. Another of whom I am thinking is quite adept at teaching study courses in a most interesting way, and it need not be stated how much of an influence she exerts. She is so outstanding in her field that she is used widely by other denominations as well as her own; and although the city in which she lives is large, she has made quite a name for herself there. When she teaches a book, she tells the name and author, and from there on never opens it for even a glance. It is truly remarkable to be able to do this so successfully. Countless other ways in which one may be of value to her church in a special way may come to mind. Dramatic ability can be used extensively, as can a gift for playing or singing. Think what a really good cook can mean when there are church dinners to prepare, or someone who sews beautifully when there are new vestments to be made.

If a minister's wife is outstanding in some way, she can mean more to her community not only as a minister's wife or a churchwoman, but as a citizen—for as such she owes something to the community of which she is a part.

There are a number of different areas in which one may find interest and pleasure. For instance, one may shine as a cook —an important role to play in a happy married life! Someone stated recently that a woman could become famous if she could cook five things well. Or suppose, possessing the particular type of personality that would appeal to youth, she excells as a worker with young people—how much this particular talent may add to her already proven usefulness! There are countless ways, of course, in which a talented woman can excel. But if she possesses no outstanding talent, she need not despair. She may learn from Robert Louis Stevenson, who wrote:

A certain sort of talent is almost indispensable for people who would spend years together and not bore themselves to death. . . . . The woman must be talented as a woman and it will not much matter although she is talented in nothing else. . . . . It is more important that a person should be a good gossip and talk pleasantly and smartly of common friends and the thousand and one nothings of the day and hour than that she should speak with the tongues of men and of angels; for a while together by the fire happens more frequently in marriage than the presence of a distinguished foreigner to dinner. . . . . You can read Kant by yourself; but you must share a joke with someone else. You can forgive people who do not follow you through a philosophical disquisition; but to find your wife laughing when you had tears in your eyes or staring when

123

you were in a fit of laughter would go some way toward the dissolution of a marriage.

In view of the influence one may exert in all these contacts and associations, it follows naturally that the value of having a particular interest or of doing some one thing well is enhanced as one becomes more expert at it. Much of the zest of life depends on doing things well. This does not necessarily mean, however, that a person must be a genius. Success at anything is due largely to effort and time plus a certain amount of talent and ability. Talent in itself is no guarantee of success! Nor is the lack of it a sure sign of failure, if it is true that success is ten per cent inspiration and ninety per cent perspiration. Some of the most interesting people in the world are not the most talented. One definition of an interesting person is "one who knows everything about something and something about everything."

Being an authority on a subject is strictly a matter of degree. One may shine quite definitely in a certain locality and go entirely unnoticed or unappreciated in another setting where competition is keener. Consider, for instance, the case of a certain young girl from a small town who was refused entrance in a school of music because, in spite of being talented, she had had the misfortune of having been trained at home by an incompetent teacher. Her inadequate background made it impossible for her at that time to stand up to the rigid entrance requirements of the school, and she was therefore not accepted. But at home—that was another question! To many people possessing less musical knowledge than she possessed, although only a student, she appeared to be an authority. Many things contributed, of course, to this feeling: sympathy for a youngster trying hard at something, recognition of her personal attractiveness, friendship for her family, and genuine respect for what seemed to many a better than average understanding of music.

Being an authority on a subject—any subject—is tantamount to being as interesting in a given field as a person can possibly be —excelling, standing out, being extraordinary. The latent talents and undeveloped possibilities of many of us should really make us blush for shame when we consider the neglect they receive. People are so busy! And often one becomes involved in trivial activities that take precious time from something else at which one could really excel. It is so easy to become stereotyped by everyday affairs.

There are many things to be considered, of course, peculiar to each situation. In the first place, it is important to consider one's health. A person who is unwell or handicapped by ill health cannot possibly dedicate herself to something which would require great time, strength, and energy. Physical capacity is the deciding factor in many an instance.

Then the financial circumstances in each case must not be overlooked. Some ministers' wives are able to afford the help of a servant; others are not. If one is burdened with too many responsibilities at one time, such as small children or invalid dependents, in addition to heavy household responsibilities, one would probably have little taste for extra duties.

One may make the well-worn plea that there is no time. This mad, mad world is so filled already with things to do and places to go. However, we must realize that people who have made a place for themselves in the sun have exactly the same number of hours at their command that the rest of us have. If we deal intelligently with our time—and fairly—we shall be forced to admit that the real crux of the matter is that of being willing to give time consistently and deliberately to a thing. We have good intentions. We make splendid resolutions each new year to do certain things, and for a few days or weeks we work hard at them. Suddenly something else of importance comes up and we let our good intentions slide for the time being—also a great deal of what we have already accomplished. Yet it is a known fact that the ability to accomplish a thing does not stand still. One goes either forward or backward. Great artists remain at the top not because of what they *can* do but because of what they *do*. The technical side alone of any profession or vocation requires constant attention and faithfulness, and the mind and spirit must be nourished to keep them at their prime. Even greatness cannot give way to indifference for even a moment. That is the price one pays for being great. Rembrandt had to paint every day to paint at all. Paderewski had to spend many hours each day at the keyboard to remain the artist he was. And so with all the other great ones.

Now to get back to lesser personalities, ourselves included. We know we cannot all be artists or professional people of high attainment. It may be that, in spite of our hidden or unused talents, we are more or less products of our environment—inescapably so. Many a person leading a quiet, uneventful life may have planned quite a different life for herself. It is doubtful that any one of us can always do the things she would like, or at which she could excel, and not be a little selfish in the matter of stealing time from something else. After all, it is strictly our own problem to decide what we can do best and to what we should give most of our time—not what somebody else thinks we can or should do. Yet, in so many more instances than we are willing to admit, we all can expand our accomplishments.

126

HER SPECIAL INTERESTS

I heard the other day of two young mothers who were discussing the question of how much time one of them should give to a certain profession in which she was admittedly an authority. The one not greatly interested in that particular subject was inclined to think that, since the other had already accomplished so much, she was foolish to waste so much time on expanding something at which she already excelled, when other things demanded so much of her attention—that the valuable time each day could be spent to better advantage at other things. Ah, Rembrandt! Ah, Paderewski!

Let us not forget the words of Paul, "Neglect not the gift that is in thee." There may be deeply important things hidden away in our lives, things of which we are entirely unaware. It also may be that the determination to create and cultivate some special interest may lead to the discovery of some hidden talent—something that would greatly add happiness and pleasure to our lives. It is not at all impossible.

XIII

HER HOBBIES

MADELEINE SWEENY MILLER

EVERY MINISTER'S wife needs a hobby. So does every fully inte-
grated personality, but the minister's wife more than most. Oh,
not a hobby in the sense of collecting mere *things!* It may be
that. But it is much more. The other day I had a letter from
a very spiritual and much-traveled poet who had always stressed
the higher values which may dominate one's personality. She
had just that day found her home completely riddled by thieves
and, in great woe, wrote, "I am in anguish! If only I could get
my jewelry back, and my fur coats, and all my precious collection from abroad! Isn't it awful? My dresses and shoes and
even my handkerchiefs are gone!" She had yet to take the
long stride revealed by Miss E. M. Almemdingen in an *Atlantic
Monthly* prize autobiography. This Russian woman, after
telling of a tragic separation of herself from her personal possessions in early girlhood, declared, "That moment a resolve was
born in me never again to get attached to any inanimate things
—parting with the least of them hurt far too much."

But hobbies need not be things. They may consist in creating beauty through one's own faculties, as John Masefield
creates his ships' models. Or they may be the accumulation of
knowledge along a specific line. It is a satisfaction to be something of an authority in some worth-while field.

The other day I suddenly asked a charming young minister's
wife, "Do you have a hobby?"

"Oh my, no!" she exclaimed, aghast at the thought. "By the time I do all that I want to do for my husband and two children, attend the church meetings, do my Red Cross work, and answer our busy parsonage phone, I have no time for any such things as a hobby."

Now really, I do not think she meant to be as self-righteous as her spontaneous reply sounded. For she added that her little girl and boy each had a hobby—one for small teacups, the other for postmarks; for canceled postmarks, she explained, are less expensive than collectors' stamps. There was, thought I, at least hope for the next generation.

This dear woman's attitude is not difficult to explain. Most ministers' wives regard their marriage vows and their pledge of Christian service as inextricably knit together. So they are and should be. But this twofold and unified commitment often leads to a prosaic and almost Pharisaic consecration not demanded by either one's husband or his parish. A narrow outlook on her calling may produce a prim, prudish wife who is neither inspiration nor comfort to her partner in the greatest of life's privileged professions. She does not stimulate him to stride forth experimentally into new fields of thoughtful investigation or even into fresh ways of recreation which send him back to his task an *enthusiastic* minister of Jesus Christ.

The poet Percy MacKaye and his wife Marion had a nightly custom of sitting before their fire for a few minutes, reading from some piece of great literature and discussing it together. Little wonder that Mr. MacKaye has dedicated a volume of his poems to the memory of his wife. The book is "a record of the union of two sensitive and poetic souls who for forty years found their greatest happiness and inspiration in each other's companionship." Kindred, these, of the two poets Browning.

129

In the prologue which Mr. MacKaye wrote and spoke at th
first performance of her drama *Emma,* based on Jane Austen'
greatest novel, he gave recognition to the art and rare huma
personality of his wife who "utterly sacrificed all things persona
to her utter devotion to me and our children." Said he, "Sh
was the zest and savor and courage of all our lives."

But how much more may parsonage husband and wife attai
to such ideal comradeship, united by the problems of thei
sacred calling and their challenges of service!

For the sake of both her own and the minister's personality
the parsoness is wise if she stops plugging her ears to the appea
ing call of some fascinating little bypath which has for year
been luring her to exploration, and for years has been passed b
for the sake of unflagging attention to the main highway o
activity. She will be enriched by poking down this byway t
explore its beauties of wayside foliage and nesting bluebird
overhead. Oddly enough, she will find that the bypath lead
in a roundabout way right back to the dear familiar scenes o
home and family. And upon her return she will find hersel
like the character in Mary Wilkins Freeman's "The Revolt o
Mother," more appreciated and more efficient for the well-love
routine. Her family will find her much more interesting be
cause she has become interested in some new and worth-whil
thing.

To the minister's wife who hesitates to take up a hobby lest i
be unbecoming to her genius for service, let me recommend
rereading of Robert Louis Stevenson's delightful little essay "A
Apology for Idlers." Do you remember his tribute to the idler'
"knowledge of life at large" as a part of the art of living? H
who looks on at the hobbies of other folk "ceases to be dog
matic, develops a great allowance for all sorts of people an

pinions." Going a step further, the gentle essayist adds: "It s surely beyond a doubt that people should be a good deal idle. . . . Extreme business . . . . is a symptom of deficient vitality; a faculty for idleness implies a catholic appetite and a strong sense of personal entity. . . . . As if a man's soul were not small enough to begin with, some dwarf and narrow theirs by a life of all work and no play; until here they are at forty, with a listless attention, a mind vacant of all material of amusement, and not one thought to rub against another, while they wait for a train." Clinching his appeal for people to become riders of energizing hobby interests, Stevenson continues: "Perpetual devotion to what a man calls his business, is only to be sustained by perpetual neglect of many other things. . . . . There is no duty we so much underrate as the duty of being happy. A happy man or woman is a better thing to find than a five-pound note." And this from the tubercular poet who gave us the joyous couplet,

> The world is so full of a number of things,
> That I'm sure we should all be as happy as kings!

Without setting himself the task of defining a hobby, the poet in his "Apology for Idlers" has given us a first-rate philosophy for it.

I have been interested in inquiring into the hobbies of other ministers' wives. One who was traveling in Switzerland became attracted to a little brass sheep bell in the village of Chamonix nestling at the foot of glacier-gowned Mont Blanc. She acquired it. At Interlaken she saw a gilded cowbell in a shop. It was adorned with a miniature painting of the Jungfrau. This her husband bought. A hobby collection of bells was born. Today she has many varieties—deep-throated,

131

sonorous camel bells from the "sûks" of Damascus; old sleigh
bells from her aunt's New Hampshire attic; church bells that
carilloned village worship; elephant bells from India, decorated
with gold and red on white; door bells; ship's bells; dainty
dinner bells; farm bells which once called the "hired help"
from the fields to consume dumplings and cabbage; a school
bell tapped by a teacher of long ago when she looked up from
her desk and called her pupils to attention.

Another parsonage friend, when her little daughter was
stricken with an incurable malady, took up the cultivation of
her lovely voice, long neglected. In the process, she not only
regained her own radiance but, unaware to herself, ministered
in a wonderful way to her discouraged husband. Many a time
as she was practicing "Ho, Everyone That Thirsteth" or "Holy
Night," her parsonage partner upstairs at his study desk sat
back and drew in courage as from a fragrant flower garden.

Another minister's wife pursues old religious books and was
lately rewarded by coming upon a two-volume set of Tissot's
portrayals of the Old Testament scenes and the life of Christ—
a very early edition with mellow color plates. "Just think,"
she exclaimed, as her husband laid down the three dollars
demanded for such a treasure in a musty Long Island cellar,
"what wonderful pageant costumes I can now design! And
what a help in teaching Bible lessons to my class! Nobody has
ever approached the accurate revelings of custom, background
and costume which Tissot brought back for the world from his
years in the Holy Land."

Another wife is gathering pieces of rare hobnail glass. Another, pewter. Another, salt and pepper shakers! Another
miniature china dogs. Another, frail glass slippers—especially
the hard-to-come-upon lavender glass slippers. Why? Why

132

knows? There is no logic to a hobby. Still another is making a collection of unusual necklaces. Unable to go to Palestine with her husband one year, she found herself upon his return the possessor of a number of fascinating little boxes. One from the Jaffa Gate in Jerusalem contained a delicate little necklace of silver filigree mulberries alternating with lumps of old lapis lazuli. Another from Istanbul held a pendant of old Turkish amber. One from Port Said contained old blue and pink faïence mummy beads from an Egyptian tomb. Traveling friends returned bearing gifts. And now this parsoness possesses a noble assortment of treasures stored in a chest of shallow drawers made by her father.

The other afternoon, in a discussion group of wives, one wistfully remarked, "I wish I had a hobby. I do not seem to collect anything but cheery little washcloths. I never can resist them when shopping in household linen departments. I am always buying them."

I found it hard to imagine having nothing but washcloths for a hobby, though one must respect the tastes of others. There are so many lovely interests in the world just waiting to be adopted as someone's hobby! Things the pursuit of whose history, whose source of origin, whose significance would broaden anyone's horizon, leading to spiritual as well as cultural adventures. Psychiatrists and medical scientists attach definite longevity values to consistent following of a constructive "outside interest."

It is quite possible for a minister's wife, busy though she be, to ride more than one hobby horse at a time. I enjoy riding several: traveling in faraway places with my husband, writing about our experiences in stories illustrated by his own lovely photographs, and the collection of rare old crosses by which the peoples of many lands have expressed their belief in the resurrection of Christ. My three chief hobbies are closely interwoven

As to my writing, I always have managed to snatch a few odd moments from other activities, not waiting for "inspiration" or for being free from noise or fatigue or interruption to set down things I feel led to express. After executing the day's meals and doing "contact work" for my Bible class or spending an hour on the telephone for the program of the women's society, I dash to my side of our huge study desk. For ever since our marriage it has been my very high honor to share the desk of my husband in our interesting study, a privilege which I have tried never to impose upon by undue disturbance of his train of thoughts. An hour spent here, pounding at my typewriter, on which I find thoughts come faster than if written down by hand, completely rebuilds my zest for the real work of our dedicated lives. Writing never tires me. It lifts me up, exalts me, in much the same way that travel through Syria, Palestine, or Egypt does, when we tramp under a sun shooting the thermometer up to incredible heights, or lean over "digs" of ancient cities with notebooks and cameras in hand.

Sitting in our study, with open bookshelves stacked to the ceiling behind me, and facing my parsonage pal as he pores over his Sunday sermon unaware of my furtive glances of admiration in his direction—sitting here, I say, looking up at the files of picture films by which we try to hold to our impressions of national groups and their home settings, or at the little museum of travel trinkets, chips of gleaming white Pentelic marble from the newly excavated Agora at Athens, or bits of burned olive wood from the city mound at Judean Lachish, or varieties of lava from smoking Vesuvius—well, writing in such an atmosphere ought to inspire something, whether it actually does or not. No wonder I consider the creation of would-be literature one of my delectable hobbies. Let me share with you my feeling for our study desk, in lines published several years ago.

OUR STUDY DESK

Our desk is like a vast plateau
Where I may go
When work is done,
And with my pen or book may run
Across the world to Borneo
And thrust myself headlong abroad
Into the universe of God.

The piles of books like mountains rise
Above the level plain where lies
A drift of sheets whose whiteness glints
Like snow awaiting fresh thought-prints.

Our desk is like a vast plateau
Where I may go
When work is done
And with my pen or book may run
Across the world to Borneo
And thrust myself headlong abroad
Into the universe of God.

But perhaps you would like me to tell you about our collection of crosses. Looking for crosses? Well, we have found plenty of them. And inspiring ones, at that. I had never contemplated making such a collection. The suddenness with which the seizure attacked me one day in precious old Athens is proof of the genuineness of the hobby. We were walking, my parson and I, among the eloquent columns of the Parthenon. A bit of broken potsherd which he saw on the ground sent us trooping down into the bazaar section of the city, near Shoe Lane, to see if we could find an ancient Greek vase at a very small price. While he was enjoying to his heart's content some red and black lecythoi from the Periclean Age, my eye wandered to a near-by case containing some junked jewelry from various Mediterranean lands.

Particularly was I attracted to a dainty filigree cross, silver gilded, and studded with rich red and dark-blue stones, cabochons typical of Byzantine beauty. From the arms of the main cross hung little pierced filigree pendant crosses. The whole was crowned with a canopy of silver. It was just such a religious symbol as a very devout lady would have worn—perhaps in some Aegean island. At my first entreaty my generous husband, who has now become the sponsor of this hobby, bought the appealing bit of religious art. Finding myself getting on so well with the new interest, I appealed to him to add the neighbor of that cross in its case—a crude old silver amulet, embossed with a hand carving of Mediterranean St. George on his horse in the act of slaying the dragon, emblem of pagan wickedness. He magnanimously added this and got his lecythoi bargained for besides. When we arrived home, we found inside the little silver box a bit of wood, a fragment of cloth, and a segment of coin—evidence that a pious peasant some two centuries ago believed he had acquired a portion of the true cross of Calvary, of the seamless robe, and of the Judas coin! Too much for our parsonage perspective on the superstitions of men! Out they came.

The two old crosses became the nucleus of a group to which we have added many others in more than one hundred thousand miles of travel in various lands, in precious peacetime. Friends and family have brought fresh specimens on high days and holy days. As we look at these, on their layers of velvet in the drawers of an old highboy, we not only relive the happy circumstances under which we found them, but are lifted up to contemplation of the redeeming work of Christ and its reflex in the art-thinking of peoples—peoples gifted and crude, rich and poor, pious and superstitious, but all reverent and yearning, expressing in these symbols in gold and silver, bronze and brass, wood and stone, coal and crystal, their desire to draw nearer to the Lamb of Calvary.

In our collection of more than 150—we aim to secure not numbers but varieties of form—we have examples of all five fundamental types of cross: the familiar Latin or Roman cross, with its unequal limbs; the square, equal-limbed Greek cross; the tau or T-shaped cross, known as the pre-Christian; the X-shaped or St. Andrew's, so named because it is believed that Andrew was crucified on a cross of that shape; and the hooked cross, or swastika, going back to very ancient Indo-European sources. They have come from twenty nations, including all the Balkan countries who have gone through the throes of national crucifixion at the hands of Hitler—Greece, Rumania, Bulgaria, and Jugoslavia. From the little buffer state of Lithuania we acquired at the World's Fair of 1939-40 a cross of Baltic amber and the replica of a wayside cross showing the carry-over of northern nature worship by the use of tiny flowers carved on the wayside shrine topped by its squatty eastern cross. Lithuania was very late receiving Christian teaching. Many of our crosses came just at the moment when the nation of its origin was going down under the cruel onslaught of destructive hate; one of our Greek crosses came the week Athens fell. A seventeenth-century Russian cross was acquired the week Nazi troops began the siege of Moscow.

Our group of Palestinian crosses, gathered on repeated saunterings among places Jesus knew, is the one we treasure most. We were amazed to find that Jericho has its local cross, looking weirdly primitive with little birds dangling from its arms and touches of coral inserted among their feathers. It is just such a cross as might come from an out-of-way place where one fell among thieves on the wilderness road. And the tiny settlement of Madeba, "over Jordan," near ancient Amman, gave us a square Greek cross studded with a dark blue stone. Most historic of Palestinian crosses is the Jerusalem or Crusaders' Cross, adopted by Godfrey, the good twelfth-century Crusader who, finding an Armenian cross, adopted it for his own, adding new significances. It is a square cross with four small square crosses inserted—the large cross signifying the wound in the Saviour's side, the four smaller ones typifying the wounds in his hands and feet. Or, said Godfrey, the five crosses stand for the five nations who went to the Crusades to rescue the sepulcher of Christ from the Moslems. The original of the Jerusalem cross of which ours is a replica, studded with red stones to denote the blood drops of the Saviour, is in the sacristy of the venerable Church of the Holy Sepulcher at Jerusalem, with the sword and spurs of Godfrey.

Our favorite Palestinian cross is, of course, the Bethlehem cross of hand-carved silver—the type proudly worn by the stalwart Christian wives of Crusader descent in the holy little hilltop town. It really does not look like a cross at all; in fact, it was oddly designed to prevent hateful Moslem neighbors from casting profane aspersions upon the emblems worn by rival religionists. It is of silver, about one and one-half inches square.

Its terminals consist of three palm leaves each—symbolizing the Trinity and, if taken all together, the Twelve Apostles. At its heart there is a star, recalling the glories of the night of the Nativity, and around the star is an encircling crown of thorns. There are spear points, reminiscent of the Roman torture. Yes. Bethlehem wears a proud cross upon its Christian heart.

Our Russian collection contains more crosses than any other but the Palestinian group. We found them principally in southern Russia, along the Black Sea, in years when the Soviets were eager to rid themselves of everything savoring of the bourgeois taste for religion. They remind us of our hours at worship in "spared" Russian churches, and they shine as symbols of a possible return to religion by the soul of the Soviets' potentially Christian peoples.

Which is the oldest in our collection? Probably the hoary bronze Byzantine cross which forms the handle of a sixth-century lamp from the Constantinople of Justinian and his successors.

And which is our favorite? Possibly the exquisite English cross from Penzance in Cornwall, made for an exhibit of silver-smiths' work. It is studded with native white topaz and trimmed with the vine and grapes symbolic of Christian unity in Christ.

But my space in this book is already used up. And I have really only begun to tell you of our inspiring hobby, or the other folk in whom we have stirred a desire to learn about the living symbol of the abundant Christ. We are happy if we have helped them or you to discover the cross as "the power of God," the pivot of life, the gift of Calvary.

XIV

HER VACATIONS

HELEN MITCHELL GIBSON

WHEN VACATION time approaches, life in the minister's family takes on a faster tempo. The stress and strain of preparation for the holiday will be felt most keenly by the wife. Clothes to wear, luggage to be put in shape, the house to be put in good order for leaving, are all tasks to which the husband will give little attention. He will be too absorbed in fishing tackle, camping equipment, the condition of the car, books to be taken along, and road maps. More than that, he will be busy making his last round of sick calls and giving helpful suggestions to families with critical illness. Death will break in on vacations in spite of all that we can do. A conversation beforehand may make it unnecessary to return for a funeral. With the parsonage closed for a month or even two weeks, provision must be made for the mowing of the lawn, the forwarding of mail, the care of the silver, Junior's paper route, and other details.

The youthful, conscientious minister's wife will be disturbed the first time that some woman in the congregation expresses the wish that her husband had a month's vacation. She will probably say it in a way to inform everyone that she thinks the minister ought not be away so long. This type of criticism is not so prevalent now as it used to be when vacations were not so common. There are those of us, however, who have to live through the year with people who feel exactly that way. We must not let them upset us. They have not stopped to think that our husbands have been on twenty-four-hour duty since the last vacation, and that it is impossible for the minister to get away from his parish responsibilities without leaving town. There are many other men who hold similar responsible positions, but there are also a great host whose work is done when the office door closes. The man who carries the load of a parish for eleven months ought to be tired when vacation time comes around, and those who appreciate his task will not begrudge him his vacation even for a month or more.

While we are on the subject of the length of vacations, perhaps it should be said that when a congregation grants a pastor a month's leave he should be careful about going away at other times. No one will register serious objection to a day off once in a while, for after all a minister's task is a seven-days-a-week proposition; but to be away too often is dishonest, and it brings dishonor to the calling in which we share.

What kind of vacation shall we take? There are many factors that will enter in, not the least of which is the condition of the bank account. Other circumstances to be taken into consideration are the age of the children, the family's health, and the kind of year that lies behind us. Every vacation should have a purpose. If rest is the main requisite, then a quiet place away from the crowds is the thing. If there has been too little in our environment to stimulate the mind, it may be that a course in some summer school will give us what we need. If our spirits have been drooping and we need a lift, a conference will work wonders. If we have been away from cultural advantages, a city with concert halls, art galleries, a planetarium, or a museum may stimulate our lives and provide table talk for the year ahead. If the world has been crowding in upon us and we have become narrow in our outlook, it may be that travel including the plains, the mountains, or the lakes will lift our horizons and broaden our outlook. If we have become burdened with life and the air is filled with knotty problems, simply a change of scenery without going far away may lift the load and clarify the atmosphere. The real purpose of the vacation is not to be away from the parish thirty days, helpful though that may be, but rather to bring the whole family back home with a new outlook on life, a refreshed feeling within, and a renewed determination to make things move during the year ahead.

It was not so many years ago that the minister's vacation was simply an opportunity for him to go back home and visit his or his wife's people. It was the cheapest kind of vacation, and it always does one good to return to the scenes of childhood. We are now living in a different kind of day; people do not visit so long in one place even among their relatives. More than that, an important part of our daily work is visiting in the homes of the parish and listening to the trials and tribulations of our flock. We need a change from this daily diet. It is not likely that we shall get it if staying at home for a month is going to necessitate calling upon all the friends of other years. All of which adds up to this: we will certainly want to visit our homes if we are not permitted to do so during the course of the year, but normally that will not be a sufficient vacation.

While thinking of this chapter, I have made it a point to inquire of parsonage friends as to the most memorable vacations which they have ever had. Almost invariably mothers will say, "I believe it was that summer when our children were half grown and we were in a cottage on the lake shore. I did not have to worry much about the family, and it was wonderful to be away from social responsibilities." Although we have been fortunate in having some delightful vacations, twice in the Colorado mountains and in travels as far west as the Pacific and as far east as the Atlantic, our children look back upon two summers spent in a simple cottage beside a quiet Vermont lake as the happiest time in their lives; and their parents heartily agree. Of course, the vacation is primarily for the pastor, and yet we do owe a responsibility to our children, and we must endeavor to make our vacation plans include something that will be helpful and stimulating to them.

Many ministers' families have bought summer cottages and make an annual pilgrimage to the same place year after year. This has the advantage of giving the children a sense of possession which they miss in the parsonage or rented house. It creates a place amid the changing scenes of pastoral rovings that to the child is permanent. Among our friends are a number who have found great satisfaction in such an arrangement. On the other hand, if one owns property and is able to be in it only three or four weeks a year, one naturally hesitates to go elsewhere for vacations. We have found a great stimulation in travel. A summer visiting the historic spots in Virginia, climaxed at Williamsburg, lingers in happy memory. A summer at the seashore with all the invigoration that comes from salt air and salt water quickens the step of the average weary vacationist. There are so many things in this country to see, that it seems too bad to tie oneself down to a definite place. If you have a bit of the wanderlust and are not wearied too much by travel, why not take a summer now and then to visit the many national parks and natural wonders in America and Canada? Perhaps there are beautiful or interesting spots very near your own parish which you ought to enjoy.

Still another kind of vacation we have found helpful is

going to some of the great religious centers like Northfield, Massachusetts; Montreat, North Carolina; Winona Lake, Indiana; Mount Herman, California; and Estes Park, Colorado. For one whose heart has become hungry for spiritual food and for stimulating Christian fellowship, there is nothing equal to it. It stretches the mind, lifts the horizon, and warms the heart. Some of our friends make such an experience a regular part of their annual vacation. For more than a generation a great host of ministers' families have traveled from far and near to Chautauqua, New York. It is a great cultural center where one can find almost everything one desires, whether it be rest, recreation, good music, or good preaching.

An exchange of pulpits is one of the common ways of taking a vacation. We have never tried it, but we know of many people who have and who seemingly have found some value in the change of scenery. If the city pastor can go to the country and live for a month in a parsonage bedecked with flowers and supported by a vegetable garden, a good time may be had by the preacher and his family. Though the pavements may be hot and the streets crowded, the country pastor and his family can find a lot of joy and satisfaction in the city manse. They will probably be glad to get back to the open spaces, but the experience in the more populous area will be a stimulus to the whole group. Probably, among those unable to afford more extensive vacations, more should be done to promote exchanges of this type that would be mutually helpful.

Naturally the preacher's wife has a right to inquire as to where she fits into this vacation picture. Is it possible to arrange it so that she can find some release from the daily grind of preparing three meals, dusting, washing, and ironing? Nothing would please a great number of us more than to go to some

144

comfortable resort and enjoy the luxury of a menu card and table service. Some in better circumstances already enjoy such luxuries; but the average budget will not permit it, at least not for long. Therefore, some other way must be found. If the vacation is to be primitive, friend husband will enjoy doing a good bit of the cooking; and if the vacation is in a cottage without a maid, the labors can be divided so that no one need be overburdened. Usually there are places to be found where one can get some meals out without overtaxing the eating account. The matter of vacation for the lady of the manse should certainly be considered in any summer vacation plans.

Suppose circumstances compel us to take our vacation at home. The new baby, a hospital experience, or Junior's summer job may require it. What then? Shall we weep and think that we have been cheated? We can, but when the month is over we shall be poor company and poorly prepared for the new year. Why not take an hour and make plans for the whole month? One day it can be a picnic in the park; another, a trip to some near-by point of historic interest; and yet another may be set aside to read some book that long has been waiting on the shelf. A friend of ours on vacation spent a most delightful day on the sightseeing bus in her own city. She enjoyed riding by familiar sights and hearing the remarks that were made about them. Others from far away enjoy such experiences. Why shouldn't we? Above all, we must make sure that home routine is different from that of the other eleven months in the year. We can eat out under the tree, breakfast on the back porch, have the washing done at the wet-wash laundry. We can play games that bring the family together, and develop those ties that have been neglected through the year. In most of our communities there are factories, mines, farms, stores, or natural wonders that we long have wanted to see but never have been able to find the time to visit. Here is our opportunity.

Some of our good friends in the church often say to us, "Have a good time and forget all about us. We will get along." Such words are a great help. It isn't always easy to forget those for whom we are responsible and of whom we are truly fond. Should we try? Or, should we keep up our parish work while away? There are ministers' wives who spend a lot of time writing letters and cards to those back home. Some make it a point to remember every family. Others write only to the sick and shut-ins. When any of this can be done without its becoming a burden, it is all right; but we must remember that we are on vacation and that anything that will prevent us from coming back to our jobs with renewed energy should be avoided.

Some self-effacing wives in our circle will stay at home and send their husbands off to see the world by themselves. There may be times when this is the thing to do. A week's fishing trip into the wilds of Canada or on the shores of the nearest lake might be something which we would not enjoy, and it might do him a lot of good. A summer conference might fill him with new ideas for sermons and give him many new suggestions for his parish work, while we probably would prefer to get away from sermons and addresses. In such a case it may be best for all concerned to let him go his way while we spend a few days in the city catching up on styles and getting ideas for house furnishings. What a joy it is to eat when and where we please! If this can be done when the children are at Scout or Y Camp, so much the better.

In the long run, however, those vacations will be the happiest and most profitable in which the whole family has heartily participated. When we were younger and had two babies at home, my husband was elected as a delegate to a meeting in Seattle. Nothing was said about my going, for with the children it seemed impossible, and besides there wasn't any money. When my husband was in the city seeing about his ticket he met an old friend. This man chided him for not planning to take me along. He said very frankly that he could not afford it, and the friend replied, "If you go alone, the trip won't mean much to you, for you will have no one to talk with about it when you come home. Take her, and it will be one of the highlights of your life." I was shocked when my husband came back all excited to report that I was going along, that he had arranged at the bank for the money. Fortunately my parents were able and glad to keep the babies. It is one of the happy memories of our lives, and no bill was paid easier. The vacations together are the ones that count for the most.

To finance the summer holiday is always a real problem. Some have not hesitated to borrow the money for it. The vacation should be looked upon as an investment in health, education, and spiritual culture. We should not hesitate, therefore, to put money into it if the return promises to be commensurate with the amount invested. We have paid for vacations before we have taken them and afterward, and have discovered that it is much more fun when we have had the money ahead of time. If you are unable to keep a balance in the bank account, why not take out a good-sized Christmas savings with the expectation of cashing it when vacation time comes? Some adopt the practice of setting aside for this purpose all extra money that comes in. If you are thrifty and plan ahead, it is remarkable what trips can be taken, and what enjoyment had, with the expenditure of very little money. Those who enjoy the outdoor life and can endure primitive living get along much more cheaply than some of us who demand more of the creature comforts. Some of our younger friends have saved expenses by renting a cottage together. This enables them to save in labor as well. Others have taken automobile trips together which reduced travel expense to a minimum. Others who have been satisfied with country life have found farmhouses where they have been able to get board and lodging at a figure not very far above what it costs to live at home. It is not easy to finance a good vacation—or, for that matter, any other capital expense—but if we really want the vacation, we shall be willing to make the necessary sacrifice for it.

We have been very appreciative of the advantages that the vacation season has afforded us. It has made a large contribution to the education of our children. Geography and history have been made more interesting. Geology and agriculture have been well demonstrated. People, places, experiences, as wall as nature's wonders, have filled the children's minds with topics for conversation and compositions. God has been found amid the glories of nature. The children know what it means to be filled with wonder and awe. My husband has not only been rested in body but also found new ideas for his work. I notice that there are likely to be more windows in his sermons after vacation, for he uses illustrations which he has picked up by the way. Vacation often provides him with a point of contact with people who come from far and near into the great city. For me it means change, something new to think about, to talk about. It means the gathering of new ideas for my home, my wardrobe, my table, and my church work. Above all else, it gives to each of us a deeper appreciation of what lies back of the parsonage door, and we return certain that no matter how humble it is there is no place for us equal to home.

XV

FROM A COUNTRY PARSONAGE WINDOW

MARY HEALD WILLIAMSON

MINISTERS' WIVES have shared for generations views from country parsonage windows. The countryside is the growing field
where young ministers first apply seminary theories to life's
realities. Most ministers' wives have established their first
homes in country parsonages. Our sisterhood has common
beginnings.

In open country crossroads, on village streets, on templed
hills, in mountain clearings, in prairie towns, and on New
England greens stand the country parsonages. The story of
their contribution to American life has never been adequately
told. The parsonage children, resourceful, with a spirit of
service, are numbered among the great. In early days, country
parsonages were both religious and educational centers. Countless biographies contain words that suggest the weight of their
influence on history.

Many believe that the view outside a window has little
effect on the task of the minister, and much less on his wife.
But the parsonage family mores of dress and food, of social
life, of children's work and play are determined largely by
the community landscape viewed from home windows. It is
true that in spiritual needs humanity speaks a universal language. The resources in cities for learning that language differ
from those in sections which the census taker and the student of

community attitudes call rural. There are differences in folk, whether they till and reap, taking the long look that comes from thinking of life processes in terms of the cycle of the seasons, or hearken to the whistle of factories and the rush of commerce.

We would not draw a sharper line between rural and urban attitudes but rather seek to present the rare and happy distinction of a view of life too long hidden because it does not spell success with dollar signs. We would not light a rosy, romantic glow in the windows of the country parsonage, but look objectively at the problems and opportunities found there, and evaluate it as a home and a base of Christian work.

No single picture could illustrate this study. The American rural scene is too varied. A common denominator is our view of growing things, of homes rooted in the seedbed of America. Each parish may have many who live on the land and work in towns, but all are united by their common concern with family and homes. In the country parish material concerns—the economics of housing, health, taxes, education, security—may loom large. But our ministry is full of even larger significances. Beneath country roofs the largest American families are reared, families that preserve their unity, and that develop resourcefulness through meeting emergencies, often with inadequate equipment. In these homes is work for all. Here are persistence and faith enough to cultivate the ground, to haul milk, to ship eggs, in good years and lean. The country parsonage home is in reality the heart of such a parish, separated from it by only a thin pane of glass, an open door.

"Your share in the foreign missionary enterprise will be that of building and maintaining a Christian home with an open door," is advice some ministers' brides receive. Such counsel applies especially to rural Christian leaders. In the country community they will be valued not for training alone, but for the home pattern which they create, the quality of daily living which they show forth.

Do you agree with the church official who said, "Look for progress when a preacher and his wife in unity face their mutual calling, when they discover the rich rewards in working together in Kingdom building"? Your call as a woman was first to a man you loved. You soon discovered the very springs of his being in his commitment to the ministry. Your own call to share that service may have sounded clear only after you learned to see through his eyes the importance of the work he had already set out to do. Unless the call has come to you personally, winning you to complete and personal consecration, you will never experience the fullness of parsonage life. If the minister's wife does not catch a sense of mission from him, who will? There is his worn black Book that you and many parishioners have seen open to words of comfort. When it becomes not only his but your most precious material possession, you have answered your call. You answer again joyously on the day when your husband receives your children at the altar, and yet again when your sons stand in pulpits of their own.

When you glimpse the spirit of a John Frederick Oberlin in your husband's eyes and undertake with him a long-time service in a country parish, then you enter upon a continuing enlargement of spiritual wealth. Your life can be rich in friends, in books, in music, in family feeling, in the joy of food from the fruit of family toil. You will be assured of work in abundance and of the need of thrift. But also you may be sure that the simple needs of health and of securing education can be met if you work intelligently and co-operatively, and "stay put." You will increasingly experience then the deep satisfactions of a

151

great calling in which you share your husband's highest aims. Problems will assume their true proportions. The pattern of your life will take form. It is not the pattern of the last mistress of the manse. It fits you, your abilities, developed and latent. It fits, too, your husband's needs from his wife, the demands of your particular family situation.

Face your call not as a minister's wife alone, but as a Christian country-woman. Look around you at the women with heavy loads of family duty who bake for church suppers, teach church school classes, keep peace in the women's group, shelter each new parsonage family. Surely a woman who goes into a country parsonage with thought only of herself will miss her rightful share in many joyous experiences of co-operative labor. Her family too will miss in her the human sweetness and growth which she should pass on to them. And little will she deserve the love lavished on parsonage folk.

We are called to be not only ministers' wives, but women of God. In what direction will our sense of mission take us? How best can we serve?

We serve first in playing our woman's role as designer of the marriage pattern. A parsonage marriage should be so glowing and radiant that it illuminates a parish. Into the design should be woven the varicolored threads of shared interests, fun, hobbies: the cultivation of good dispositions; the substitution of friendly counsel for the criticism that destroys naturalness and poise; quiet decisions as to finances and private facing of hardship; keen desire in each to give and mutual sharing to enrich that giving; adequate rest; friendship with relatives-in-law; candlelight, growing companionship, love graciously expressed. Running through the design will be the golden thread of dedication to a common Saviour and Cause.

Keep up appearances. Let your people know the true colors of your pattern. One minister and his wife recall a shock and a lesson they received. Between them they knew their marriage was all-satisfying. Yet they overheard a parishioner say, "Isn't it a shame! They are grand folks; but why is he so cross with her, constantly criticizing and correcting her; and why is she such a nagger?" Give your partner a "good build-up" based on your thorough appreciation.

"If I could start again," one minister's wife said, "I would exchange that summer of graduate study for an apprenticeship in Mrs. Davis' kitchen." So say many of us who moved into country parsonages fresh from city or school. Consider Mrs. Davis. She uses wood from the farm, and a pitcher pump, but such meals as she sets on the large kitchen table! She is no slave to dirt or to work. Her hands are well trained; her work is organized. It is her joy, but it can always wait when the pastor asks her to call down the road. The young folk pull taffy and pop corn in her kitchen. A minister's wife may learn this graceful kind of efficiency.

A minister's wife should learn too that country folk use what they have, that wise ones live largely from the land and pay as they go. Do you know the thrill of making a pat of your own butter? Then, as your feed bill mounts, you will learn how to enter with your parishioners into the milk problem. Caring for animals is good for parsonage children, for the family budget, and for the important habits of going to bed and getting up in the country parsonage!

Membership in the extension clubs for women brings knowledge of canning, of nutrition, and of many practical ways of country living. Too few country ministers' wives are active in this great adult educational movement of the rural community.

There is a distinct relationship between short pastorates and parsonage repairs. Be patient. If you stay, the bathrooms and kitchen cupboards will come. Many of us have experienced the devotion of country women who, lacking these conveniences in their own homes, sacrifice and work to modernize that of the minister, "because the parsonage is a busy place, and it must be convenient."

Remember those first summers when with great enthusiasm and equal inexperience you indulged in awkward papering of high ceilings? You determined to develop in your people a sense of pride in their property, and to improve the parsonage for them. Ministers' families should be Christian tenants, practicing stewardship in the care of material goods. They should care well for parsonage grounds. It is sad, in rich fruit sections, to find grounds used by parsonage families for over a century, and no fruit. The attitude has been, "It isn't worth the work. We'll never eat the fruit or pick the lilacs." A sense of mobility and impermanence has too often characterized the country ministry.

Often the necessity of maintaining a "front" has meant trying economics and lack of equipment. Remember those leaky tubs? Aren't a good washing machine, a pressure cooker, and other labor-saving devices more important than the coveted overstuffed furniture? Invite the extension agent to hold a kitchen conference and suggest inexpensive improvements to be made by the parish men.

Resourcefulness plus a cultivated sense of color can make of the country parsonage a charming home. Don't scorn the antiques. Refinish them. Go to auctions; they are great fun and genuine country institutions. Old glass, corner shelves, slip covers, fresh ruffled curtains framing a country view, homemade dressing tables, growing plants—these can be your. There is candlelight when day is gone, with books, magazines, music, the "lived-in look" that children bring to a home. Here are the elements for simple gracious living. We can point the way, when war times are over, to those who will seek such satisfactions, such treasures of simplicity. We are in the advance guard if we have found genuine happiness in the blending of these simple elements, in the recognition that creating from them a restful home is a major portion of our calling.

Let yours be a home that is a center, not only a circumference, a home with such a rich, friendly, and happy spirit that the very walls bulge out with the joy of living. It is this spirit of home that touches even the roads of the world where the weary and hunted wander. This spirit is compounded of many things that the parsonage home can give in abundance. If there are times when the church must come first, there should be also hours when nothing can take precedence over the family. One parsonage family have taught their parish to respect "family sings" every Sunday at four. Others observe Sunday candlelight hours during Advent, when the crèche is the center of song and story. There are Easter sunrise breakfasts, impromtu picnics. There is high celebration on birthdays and at all festive times. There is the early start for church on Communion Sunday, with family prayers on a hilltop. It is not alone the marriage pattern but the family one that preaches a sermon on the Christian home!

The parsonage family must maintain a sense of partnership in the family enterprise. There must be understanding, not resentment over the loss of father's hours at home. Rejoicing over his home-coming, the family may make so much of the time together that its value far outweighs the measure in hours.

Family partnership is built not only in festivals, but in common work experiences. Pride in the good work of hands, skill in manipulation, ability to take what life offers, stamina—all can be developed in country living.

Social scientists know that active participation in religion by both husband and wife is vastly important to well-adjusted marriage. Family religion plays a leading role in building family spirit. It is hard to separate work, play, religion, if the family altar is movable and each day is heightened by sincere worship. Guiding children to leadership in home worship built on the common experiences of wonder and joy, need and sorrow, means the discovery of new resources, the rooting of habits for individual prayer and spiritual growth in the whole family.

In Glenn Clark's book *I Will Lift Up Mine Eyes* is this dedication: "To Louise, whose simple, beautiful life has made our home a sanctuary where the sorrowing may find comfort, the erring may find forgiveness and the lonely may find love." Here is an expression of qualities which make an ideal home with an open door. Central in the parsonage ministry is a sense of hospitality, consisting, Emerson remarks, of "a little fire, a little food, and an immense quiet." Let the hospitality be the kind visitors will enjoy. They may even share in the plans and in providing the food. Unless the entertainment is simple, saving time, money, energy, then hospitality may become drudgery and a cross.

There was a young wife who, fresh from seminary days, planned an "at home." She took none of the parish women into her confidence. She set the hour at four. Her husband, also new to country life, failed with her to realize that women's affairs create a transportation problem and that four o'clock is about chore time. The phrase "at home," written into the invitation, is foreign to the rural community. No one came to the bride's "at home." The wedding china and the dainty sandwiches were untouched. Today the bride, grown older, has forgotten most of the hurt, analyzed the experience, and learned from it to adapt her hospitality to ways of country living.

Young people, especially those with insecure family backgrounds, need often to plan for buffet suppers, wash the dishes, and frolic in the parsonage kitchen. Soon they will feel at home and find the open door of the parsonage in times of heartache and joy, bringing high moments of a rewarding ministry. They will catch too a vision of a home where happiness is not measured in possessions but in close-knit compainionship and mutual sharing. They will learn to imitate a parsonage hospitality which cuts across barriers of class that often exist in the country as in the city community.

Not long ago, the countrywomen in one parish wanted a parsonage ministry. They told the new minister so. They wanted a parlor where they could talk to the minister's wife as well as the study where her husband could be found. They wanted a room always ready for weddings. With their own hands they papered and painted that parlor. The record to date is fourteen weddings at the altar they helped to build!

We visited in the home of one of America's greatest preachers. The efficient, orderly study, the parish maps, the large files, spoke of fourteen years' achievement in an ever-widening field. The desk of the minister's wife, with carefully chosen books, many for use in the devotional period, spoke of her ministry. A fireplace was in the making, one of a succession of improvements. There was a large room set aside for games and reading of the community young people. Money alone could not reproduce the atmosphere of this home that had literally grown out of the service and devotion of pastor and wife for their people. One knew that here the first quest had been for the Kingdom, that the necessities had come slowly and surely. In this home are developed socialized young people, with an outgoing enthusiasm for life, youth who have never known a boring day, who will always be at home with all groups. Here is a home that will be little affected by depressions or by the severest crises. It is founded on abiding values.

There is one door that the minister's wife should keep closed. That is the study door. A great difference in our parsonage life, city and rural, lies in the fact that the country minister's study is usually in his home. In the country, work is heavier, labor-saving devices are fewer. The wife of the minister faces a constant temptation to call him away from the shortest part of his day, his morning for prayer, study, and planning. But cannot the chores be saved until lunch time? It is easy for the mistress of the parsonage to let a bump of self-pity grow as she scrubs away, wishing she could have just one morning to sit down. She should trade places with her husband and plan a worship service, telling her husband to call her as often as she does him. She would then learn that one's best work cannot be done with the dread of interruption hanging constantly over one. Even enlightened self-interest demands that the minister have uninterrupted time to plan his sermons and to build a balanced church program. His mornings in the study bring blessing to his home. Should his wife be troubled and anxious when his daily communion with God rules the life and decisions of the man in the study?

Does she seem a paragon, this minister's wife? She needs to

be; there is no apology for expecting much of her. She can meet her life only if she too has a place set apart and carries with her the spirit of her quiet times, practicing the Presence continuously. She must keep sharp and keen her awareness, growing in her understanding of Jesus' way of life, growing in her powers of evaluating and choosing. She must grow in the organization of her work. Her body must be as well and strong as possible, her spirit free from harbored resentments.

"Once I was frightfully sensitive. Now if I feel someone has mistreated me, I quickly find a natural reason for talking with him, asking his help or advice. I have no time to waste on rancor or self-pity. So often I have found that I have mistaken others' motives and meanings." These are the wise words of one who is growing daily.

The minister's wife should grow in her ability to be objective. Early in our ministry, I came home in tears from a Ladies' Aid meeting. My wise husband said, "Mary, we can't serve if you're going to do this very often. We are here to help people. If one way doesn't work, we'll try another. Remember the chemist in the laboratory. If the first combination doesn't yield the desired result, he doesn't cry about it. He takes careful notes on his method, observes his mistakes, and tries again. His personal feelings enter very little into his course of action."

One must grow where it is hardest, in one's weaknesses. One must strive for maturity, grow up emotionally, face life instead of running from it. The hardest tasks should be done first. Everybody should be as "oil to the flame of one's love." One need not talk business, the statistics of miles of meetings. And there is no limit to the good one will do if one doesn't care who gets the credit! Above all, one should grow in the ability to combine a praying heart with serving hands.

It is difficult to separate the two sides of a pane of glass; they belong together. You cannot have a lovely view from the inside of your window unless the outside is shiny too. You cannot maintain a home, least of all a parsonage home, as an island. One of your husband's greatest needs is a wife who is an intelligent listener and counselor. To meet that requirement you must not only respect his confidences, but know the rural American scene. His problems then will straighten out in the telling, because he has an intelligent listener.

Today the trees and hills, the mountains and prairies viewed from country parsonage windows appear changeless and abiding. But a new vocabulary among rural leaders is evidence of the changing rural scene. Here are headline topics in any story of today's rural life:

School-bus behavior—traveling library—migrant beanpickers—Farm Security Administration needs church basement for mattress project—freezer lockers vs. pressure cookers—folk-game festivals—farm women's camp—refinishing furniture lesson—milk strike—4-H achievement day—dust bowl and conservation—Lord's acre movement—pecan co-operative—Larger Parish formed—rural electrification meeting—farms bought by the government—land to be used for munitions dump—backwash of youth expected in country communities after the war.

The minister's wife can realize her opportunity for enriching rural life only through an appreciative attitude toward the changing scene of country people and their significance. Rural life may become her hobby. She may read the novels of today which tell of country life. She may discover the beauty spots of reality in the countryside around her. Do you know the history of your community? Do you know what gift of life it has made to the world? Do you know where the village industries are? Do you know the beauty of rural handicrafts, in the South, around the world, hidden in your own community? Do you know folk music, folk tales and games? Do you know the joy of joining other women in creative activities for the good of the country community?

If one would understand and love life in the country, one must learn to value the small satisfactions. If the minister's wife is an artist in music, in color, in expression through writing, she will find no symphony concerts or art galleries; but she will find hungry people, often with outstanding gifts and training, waiting for larger opportunities. She will not find, perhaps, an accompanist for difficult solo work, but she will find girls who need encouragement in their music, folk who would welcome a community chorus. She will learn, often through disappointment, that country folk change slowly their ideas and traditions; they may go along outwardly on a program introduced by pressure and enthusiasm, but if it has not sprung from them—from ideas, it is true, that she may have planted—it will mean little. The minister's wife must not be in a hurry, not even to get home after the church suppers and the grange meetings. Country folk like to visit. She must be *in* the community. She and her husband must not run away to other preacher friends for all their pleasures. If she is lonely, other couples may be too. She may well be the one to gather a group of them together to play and laugh, to work at crafts, and to talk about the family life.

We in the country church can furnish the motive power for building the world of tomorrow in the countryside. Country-life organizations are numerous. They need "shepherding." Many of the terms in the new rural vocabulary express national concern over the farmer's economic plight. But economic improvement alone will not produce a better nation. It is only a genuine sense of Christian brotherhood that prevents good times from producing fatness and selfishness of souls.

One of the most hopeful signs on the rural church horizon is a group of well-trained younger ministers, in every denomination and state, dedicated to a lifetime rural ministry, working not only in country pulpits but with state councils, and furthering co-operative movements such as those of the Larger Parish and the Federated Church. In the country parsonages of America live women who are co-workers with their husbands in these significant adventures. Such people are the best evidence that a long-time ministry from a good minister of Jesus Christ produces fruits of the spirit. To many American churches which are great but not big, students beat a path, lured by a tale of a quality enterprise, even as the world has beat a path to the village of Oberamergau to witness the achievement of other country folk who present a spiritual interpretation of life.

In rural America, which is the seedbed of the nation, the mistress of the country parsonage in her unique way makes her daily contribution to transforming and developing life within and without the country parsonage windows.

XVI

I MARRIED A RABBI

RUTH WOLF LEVI

I AM THE wife of a rabbi. This seems a simple statement, but there is far-reaching meaning in the term "a rabbi's wife," or "a minister's wife." It is not like saying, "I am a grocer's wife" —a grocer has *his* customers—or, "I am a lawyer's wife"—a lawyer has *his* clients—or even, "I am the wife of a doctor"— because in large degree the physician serves a following that distinctly belongs to him. The situation is different with the minister. He is avowedly the servant of the public; and his wife, if she is animated by the desire to be a co-worker in his profession, if she shares his high ideals and would give her utmost to uphold him in every fine endeavor, must set herself with firm resolution to be like "perfect music unto noble words." She must in generous measure, though somewhat indirectly, also be a servant of the public. She must not be a "clinging vine," a dependent wife, and even the children must not be possessive, that the husband and father may be free to serve people and causes at all times, unhampered by what is the accepted meaning of the expression "a family man."

I have been the wife of a rabbi for almost thirty-five years, but I remember as distinctly as if his words had been addressed to me only yesterday the advice of the beloved clergyman who officiated at our marriage. I was approaching it with reluctant feet and apprehensive mind because I feared that independent action and the ministry could never join. When I shared my doubts with this wise rabbi and friend, he said, "Have no mis-givings as to the responsibilities that await you. Your first and greatest duty always will be to look out for the welfare of your husband. Naturally a community will place many burdens upon his shoulders. Let it be your first interest to see that he does not go beyond the limit of his strength. People cannot see another individual clearly when their own needs are in-volved or in their ardent championship of what to them are great and worthy causes. Communities have a way of over-working their ministers. Have a care."

Now this counsel could well apply to the wife of every minister possessed of consecrated ideals and determined to serve his people and his community in a selfless way. It is ever her part to put on the brakes gently but firmly, to conserve her husband's strength, yet at the same time to stimulate him to put forth his best efforts for people's welfare; for she can help him greatly in separating the important from the trivial. It is ever her part also to keep alive his ambition for his own mental development, and to help him maintain constantly the highest ethical ideals in his personal life as in his contact with the community. But the rabbi's wife is peculiarly aware of such responsibilities because of the history of her position.

In ancient days the rabbi's wife enjoyed no privileges and knew no responsibilities where the synagogue and the larger world outside were concerned. The rabbi was both religious leader and tradesman; but his wife was not connected with his business, nor was she permitted to take part in his charitable activities. She was deprived even of the privilege of marketing, as that duty also was accomplished by the rabbi. Her entire world was found within the home—as was the case with all Oriental women—and she did not move in society outside her family circle. The traditional attitude toward women was such as to make her self-effacing, and she was taught to remain always in the background. As the famous Rabbi Johanan expressed his attitude toward marriage, "One could not study the Law with a millstone around his neck." In the Middle Ages, there was a little opening of the door, but still women were rigidly excluded from active participation in public worship, and the rabbi's wife was no exception. By the sixteenth century, at rare intervals some greatly gifted woman achieved freedom in charitable work; but no reference can be found to any rabbi's wife's ever being permitted outside responsibility or the enjoyment of synagogue honors.

Yet even in olden days the evidence is that the rabbi's wife was not a "millstone." For example, much importance was attached to the personal appearance of the rabbi, and it was expected that he should always be dressed so as to command respect. Rabbi Johanan said, "The Rabbi should appear as clean and pure as an angel." The rabbinical attire was generally a long flowing white robe over which was often worn a gold-trimmed official coat. Since there were no washing machines in ancient days, it is easy to visualize at least one indispensable function of the rabbi's wife. The fact is that not only was it permissible for a rabbi to marry; he was expected, even required, to take a wife. This worked immeasurably toward the elevation of the married state. Great hospitality was the rule in rabbinical homes, and the entertainment of poor students was especially stressed. The home of the rabbi grew to be the center of a cultured circle and was the pattern after which other homes modeled themselves.

Gradually, very slowly, came the evolution in the life of the rabbi's wife. Once denied even the privilege of witnessing synagogue worship and activities, her entire world limited to what she could make of her home and family life, today she has passed through the wide-open door. She not only participates in public prayer, but along with all the women of the congregation fulfills many obligations in the work of the synagogue. And many other avenues of serviceableness are open to her. There is a bewilderment of opportunity. It is not only her privilege but her obligation to work for the general good. But her first duty is still crystal clear: she is the rabbi's wife.

Next to her home activities, the chief obligation of the rabbi's wife is definitely to assist in the work of the synagogue over which her husband presides and to interest herself wholeheartedly in the people he serves. This must take precedence over any other cause outside her home. But gone is the day when the rabbi's wife was restricted to the elemental tasks of her household and the synagogue. She still has home, family, and synagogue; and since so great a part of the Jewish religion is domestic in essence, she gives those three her greatest reverence and complete loyalty. But in our day one could hardly enumerate the responsibilities she may assume—the privileges for service she may claim as her own. Denied self-expression for many years, she now has opportunities crowding so thick about her that she must be wise to select those causes which she is best equipped to serve.

For the wife of a rabbi in a metropolis there is a very pressing immediate need for action. It is to alleviate, as far as lies in her power, the overwhelming distress of the women among the newcomers to our country. What I refer to is not the want of shelter, food, clothing. These necessities are well cared for by generous people and practical committees. But what of the cry of the dispossessed soul? These emigrés, who have come in an endless stream, are in as much distress of soul as of body. Rabbis carry such burdensome programs that they cannot dedicate themselves to this added great need. Moreover, it takes a woman to understand women; so perhaps these representatives of a lost generation can be helped in a spiritual way by the rabbi's wife. The complete program of aid is not clear because of the overwhelming numbers of the newly arrived. But is it not better to comfort, to sustain, to fan the almost extinct spark of faith in God and belief in human kindliness in a few people than to ignore the need altogether? Not only *can* those women whom one can contact be helped, but they *must* be if they are to be saved religiously. It has been said, "He who saves but one soul is counted by the Rabbis as having saved the whole world."

We have come upon a time in which we are inclined to think in terms of masses, large groups, whole peoples; and to regard individuals, their problems, their ultimate destiny as unimportant. This is a grievous social loss, but people in our time have had their minds all but forced into an acceptance of the belief that personal destiny is insignificant. The rabbi and his wife cannot be satisfied with such a philosophy. They may not lose sight of the fact that, no matter what goes on in this great, sad, troubled world, the life of each person is of value. In the normal development of human nature, each person seeks happiness and copes with difficulties of many kinds. The rabbi will be called upon for help in every elemental problem, in every major occurrance in the life of his parishioners. He, and with him his wife, must try to keep a sense of proportion, of human dignity, and of the sanctity of personality.

Because this is so, there is nothing more important for a minister's wife than a well-developed sense of humor. She

167

should of course have compassion and try to serve those in distress, but she must also be able to see the amusing side of things in order to keep a normal outlook. If very sensitive to the pain of the world and carried away by her reaction to it, if helpless to change sad conditions for better ones, she will, unless she has the leaven of humor, be depressed, dejected, incapable. There are innumerable amusing episodes to brighten up the cloudy days like sunshine, and she should try to enter into these incidents with enjoyment. Not only will she be in better mood thereby to meet straining situations and more helpful to those who need her friendly solicitude, but she will be a better companion for her minister-husband. Disturbed, distressed at life's inescapable harshness, and harassed that he can do little more than listen with pity and counsel to the limit of his wisdom, he needs a light-hearted companion, one with whom he can relax and find recreation, one who can dispel the gloom that envelops him from daily contact with defeat, depression, disillusionment. The "tired businessman" is a byword, but who ever thinks in a similar way of "the tired minister"? Well, the wife who witnesses the wear and tear can and should plan for a lessening of the strain.

Scarcely less important than humor and good cheer is the necessity of developing an interest in something entirely removed from the routine of the ministerial life. Being engrossed in some secular project will not only enrich life, but keep the minister's wife from being entirely used up by her husband's work and obligations. This interest can be anything that appeals: the love and study of art, an educational effort, gardening, collecting and working for a hobby, or—my own choice—the abiding love for and appreciation of music. Music has been my second great love; and, like the first, it can be recommended as one of the enduring satisfactions of life. Most interests fade and fail as the years multiply, but age only deepens one's joy in music.

So it must be admitted that one married to a minister has a more complex existence than other women experience. As I look backward, the vista of the years presents a mosaic in which complications and compensations are inlaid to create the complete picture. The advantages seem greater in number, and it is a simple matter to point out some that are outstanding. Without any effort on her part, beyond keeping alive a sincere interest in them, the minister's wife knows from the outset a large circle of friendly people. She is the possessor of an educated, religious, cultured companion who can help her to a higher personal level of development, mentally and spiritually. Since the rabbi is the representative of his people and his presence is sought everywhere where communal problems are being solved, the wife also has the opportunity, though in less degree, to use her influence for developing a better understanding of her people, more especially among the women in church groups and women's organizations. If the rabbi's wife loves young people—and what one does not?—she has the privilege of witnessing the unfolding of their lives, of being close to them in their joys as in their trials, of affecting their decisions in important matters regarding their welfare—in short, when her sympathetic understanding attitude is known to them, she may become their confidential friend.

In trying to do justice to the advantages that are part of the ministry, one must pay tribute to the generous, thoughtful attitude that the congregation assumes in regard to every outstanding event in a minister's home. There is such a whole-hearted response in the hearts of many of the congregation when some joyous incident happens. This sharing of happiness with the minister's family truly deepens their rejoicing and satisfaction. The arrival of a little one is of so much interest and pleasure that it might well be considered a congregational child. And in hours of strain, of trial and sorrow, the congregation seems like one big family, proffering assistance, extending sympathy, hearts echoing to the grief that has been experienced or the loss that has been sustained, doing everything possible to lessen the heartache and strengthen those in sorrow. Truly this is a compensation that far outweighs any difficult congregational experience that could be part of the life of a minister's wife.

What is on the other side of the shield? One of the outstanding liabilities is the lack of privacy. Perhaps it is inevitable, but in a minister's home the wife often feels that she is living in a goldfish bowl. Whether her existence is in a small city or a metropolis, the only difference is in the size of the bowl. And she is called upon always to be hospitable, amiable, friendly, and above all tactful. I can think of no woman who needs more tact. She has little leisure, for anyone in a large group can command at will her attention, and time. Also she loses one of life's satisfactions in that she may not be a part of a single group or develop an intimate circle. It is open to discussion whether it is an asset or a liability to be placed so that one hears both sides of many current tales and must always show discretion—must seem to know nothing of the matter under discussion. Another of the great disadvantages in the position of the rabbi's wife is that people are not quite themselves with her. She longs for a more relaxed informal attitude, wants to feel that she "belongs"; but, with few exceptions, there is a constraint in people's demeanor which keeps her a stranger among them, even after many years.

Many years ago, seeking the guidance that the experience of one much older might give, and eager, uplifted, and hoping for the inspiration that would flow from one still enamored of her place in life, I approached at different times two veterans in the field. Upon asking the advice of one rabbi's wife, I received the reply, "My dear, whatever you do, you will regret." From the other the answer was, "Whatever you do, you will be criticized—so please yourself." Devastating!

Every minister's wife is naturally subject to criticism. She is conscious of this and cannot be callous to the knowledge. The women of the congregation, much more than the men, will pass judgment on her, and those outside the fold will also analyze her. Public opinion is thrown on her with a pitiless light, and this with little real knowledge of the person under discussion. If she is brilliant or militant or persuaded of her ability to be a leader, she is likely to be considered forward, aggressive; if she is timid, hesitant, or just convinced that it is wiser that only her husband's voice should be raised in the market place, she will be called stupid or lacking in initiative. If she has a keen interest in style and modishness and looks as if she had stepped out of *Vogue*—and some ministers' wives are lovely to look upon—she will be said to be vain and frivolous; if she considers extreme stylishness trivial and unworthy the time it requires, her criticis will pronounce her dowdy, "old-timey," obsolete. If she naturally has a fondness for social functions and maintains an intimacy with rich or powerful people, she will definitely be called a "climber" and snobbish; if, on the other hand, she prefers people to personages, society to Society, she is sure to be regarded as indifferent or unsocial. If only the synagogue or church would realize that the organization comprises many persons, that the minister's wife is but one, and that by reason of many inevitable congregational duties her time is limited and her program full, these fault-finders would become more lenient in judgment and more understanding.

Perhaps the most trying feature of a ministerial home is that it becomes the "listening post" for endless sad stories. I have often wondered what there is in human nature that persuades people to come so readily, so eagerly, so constantly to the rabbi's home in their trying hours and so seldom to report the cheerful episodes in their experience. Why so much relating of tragedy and so little telling of joyous, heart-warming events? It would seem that the rivers of sadness flow wider than the rivers of joy. But we who have lived long know this is untrue. It is just that people take their blessings for granted and are overwhelmed by the adverse happenings that overtake them.

If, as history informs us, the wife of the rabbi put most of her energy and found all of her inspiration in her home, then one might say with accuracy that the room in which family and friends gathered would reflect her personality more than any other part of the house. The study, the library—these bear the mark of her husband, the scholar; but the place where the family assembles, whether for prayer or play, would seem to be peculiarly the center of existence for the wife, the mother, the mistress of the home. It has been said that "walls have ears." If it were true that they also have tongues, what tales our living room could tell! Here could be heard a many-sided story of existence—the narrative of a cross section of life!

These listening silent walls have absorbed stories of laughter and tears, of children at play and grown-ups under stress and strain, of young girls confessing a dream of and hope for the love of some favored one and marriage attesting the dream come true, of young mothers proud and happy with their little ones, of parents and children unhappy because of misunderstanding each other, of domestic infelicity, of heartbroken widows, of old people depressed because of lack of income and so deprived of their physical comfort, of men and women still strong and able but unemployed, of bright and ambitious students, of cynical youth, of weddings breathing happy circumstance, of brides with eyes downcast because of heavy hearts and foreboding of the future, of troubled foreign-speaking souls, of beggars insistent in their demands, of books discussed, of arguments indulged in, of music performed, of refugees confused and despairing—*ad infinitum*. These silent, patient walls bear witness to a "heap of livin'," to the sympathetic helpfulness of a wise rabbi and to the eager interest of a rabbi's wife.

A brilliant man once said to me, "There is only one position more difficult to fill than that of a minister, and that is being the minister's wife." I disagree, for in my opinion the difficulties of the position are more than outnumbered by the advantages. For many years I have been on the side line, watching an unselfish servant of God and man take part in the battle of life for all who turned to him for help in the fight. To be a minister's wife is an outstanding privilege—a blessed responsibility. To be allowed intimate contact with people in their joys, to be permitted to share in their sorrows, to help comfort the heartsick and dry the tears of grief, to be the confidante of young people in their search for happiness, in their pursuit of personal development or consecration to some unselfish cause—these things enrich life. If a young girl should ask my advice now regarding marriage to a clergyman, I would say, "Go ahead if this man is indispensable to your happiness, but you must love him a little more than if he were a layman."

XVII

SAINTS AND LADIES AND MINISTERS' WIVES

MARGARET T. APPLEGARTH

You CAN almost always tell a saint from a lady. Not so much on account of the halo of the one, as on account of the hat of other—the lady's having considerably more style. But sometimes a minister's wife leaves you guessing as to which is her status; and that is probably sensible of her, since she may need leeway enough to experiment with all sides of her character; for it takes longer than you think to discover what a disturbing career is hers.

Unless she is born in a manse, the minister's bride, as I see her, little suspects either the pitfalls or the pinnacles of her fate! Listen to her matron of honor, who almost invariably says: "Aren't you the lucky girl? To be going off to a strange city with hundreds of ready-made people all set to receive you with open arms, and even a parsonage all swept and garnished. It wasn't like that when I married my insurance man, I assure you. Not a soul in the whole place knew or cared that we had arrived; and as for a house, we scoured the town before finding a single roof we could afford."

Yet the fact of the matter is that it would be better to warn the minister's bride: "You poor unfortunate woman, don't you realize that you are about to move into a glass house? Because it belongs to the congregation, and you belong to the congregation too, the parsonage takes on all the transparency of an

174

aquarium; and while you may feel gloriously 'in the swim' from the moment you first float into it, just realize that you can never hope to have the pleasant privacy which the most insignificant insurance man can guarantee his wife. As long as you live, this fishbowl of yours will be watched by its church owners with conscientious curiosity. On almost any day goldfish will come floating in at high tide, graciously donating this or that gadget for which you must always be duly grateful; weakfish will be carried in at very low tide indeed, in search of backbones; bluefish will color all the atmosphere for hours at a time with the most gloomy indigo hue; whitefish will faint in coils all over the parsonage floor; whales will heave themselves indoors, spouting with pride and prejudice, and incidentally swallowing all your poor Jonahs. Are you prepared to cope with such a procession of small nightmares, all the time under public scrutiny?"

"I am prepared!" the little bride boasts blithely, and moves into her aquarium to live happily ever after. Yet it is no fairy tale. For nobody ever waves a magic wand at perilous moments, or warns her beforehand that, should her cup run over, the trustees will undoubtedly postpone redecorating and painting.

And speaking of decorating, the initial problem is: What kind of an Exhibit A shall this glass house become? At this point the saint and the lady have very different desires.

Not long ago one young minister's bride had a memorable conversation with her father-in-law. "My dear girl," he began, "before you buy a single thing for your new home, do remember that from now on you are going to be supported by persons with far less salary than you and Bill will receive. So I beg of you not to have such a glamorous modern house that all the women in the church will feel dissatisfied at once with their own stodgy well-known stuff. Suppose they begin pestering their husbands for exciting effects like yours! Suppose this not only alienates the menfolks but even militates against your popularity! Suppose that when the husbands yield, the church offerings grow less! Remember that for years to come you and Bill will be living in a world where nobody is going to have quite enough money to go around, what with paying for old wars and for new ones. Think of the deep poverty ahead of too many people; think of the temptation to sacrifice benevolences first and keeping up with the Joneses last of all. I don't want you to represent the Joneses!"

"Dear me!" groaned the little bride, seeing herself headed for sainthood reluctantly. She felt the halo getting tangled up with orange blossoms, and continued brightly, "How odd that mother should be talking with Bill about this very thing, right now!"

Odd enough! And another straight talk: "Now, my dear boy, you must realize that ministers no longer have quite the prestige they had when I was a girl; the trouble seems to be that the ministerial *status quo* has stayed behind, while the rest of American living has raised its standard—radio, movies, advertisements all setting a modern pace. So here's my Nancy, brimful of culture and aesthetic ideas, aching to make your parsonage a center of such charm and beauty that every young person in the congregation will be lured to it as if by magic. And when they go out to form homes of their own, Nancy's exquisite taste and Nancy's interpretation of creative living will loom before them as a pattern. Just ask yourself if pokey left-over sticks of furniture from your father's attic will ever excite a single young girl to copy Nancy? For mercy's sake, Bill, use your eyes! If God goes to such daily trouble over sunsets, flowers, and butterflies, surely a creative glory ought to emanate from a minister's home too!"

The lady, you see, was beginning that perennial tussle with the saint, a tussle out of which every minister's wife discovers toward the end of her life whether she is ascetic or aesthetic at heart. Meanwhile the congregation gazes spellbound into the glass house, noticing the provocative results of unknown and diverse warnings, appreciating obvious hand-me-downs— "Plenty good enough to begin with!"—from every relative on both sides of the family set shoulder to shoulder with the disturbing new choices which everybody greets with "Oh!" and "Ah!"—just as the bride's mother had predicted—which undoubtedly will lessen the offerings when various unofficial observers break the commandment about covetousness, eventually spending their substance in riotous duplicates—just as the new father-in-law had anticipated.

This is a pitfall that usually occurs only at the beginning of clerical life. The truth of the matter is that a minister resembles a farmer or a lighthouse keeper, and should not go out hit or miss to pick a wife just because she has a bewitching freckle on her nose or an amazing way of dimpling when she talks. If the farmer needs someone with specialized and homely skills —such as ability to cook en masse for farmhands and a general kindness to dumb animals, plus an inherited understanding of how to make both ends meet in lean years—how much more the minister needs these very qualities raised to their nth degree in his lady, a lady always with one eye on the crop and another on the weather, in complete co-operation with his seasonal duties. And if a lighthouse keeper needs a woman who can patiently take isolation in overlarge doses, who can tend a lamp for better or worse, for richer or poorer, in storm or in calm, all for the sake of saving some poor sailor on some dark night, how much more the minister needs these very qualities magnified to a spiritual level in the keeper of his parsonage.

As if combining the traits of two such demanding husbands were not enough for one woman, the minister's wife adds those of a third man also, with a more baffling role to play. For a farmer rarely pulls up stock and barrel to go off to a far-flung field in another state, and a lighthouse keeper stays put on the rocks; but an army officer is moved like a pawn from east to west, from north to south, and his wife knows constant shiftings. Hers not to reason why. "He" has been called; so out come excelsior, barrels, crates, as she begins the gallant and ghastly ordeal of packing. From the army angle, a crop and a rescue seem like simple rational procedures indeed compared to the training of a rabble regiment, half the time made up of people who have neither volunteered nor been drafted, but who just drift along because they rather like the company and don't mind the dress parade once a week—if it doesn't rain. But what a curious army is that in which, when the captain calls "Onward!" the Christian soldiers go sidewise, should they feel like it; an army in which discipline is taught in the gentlest of weekly doses, lest there be too many discouraged deserters; an army in which all ages and sexes, as well as the lame, the halt, and the blind, march forward side by side—when they do march. The wife of such a leader must be drilled into shape herself very early in the game—to accept hardship and short rations for the glory of the cause, to exert influence and initiative for the honor of the Kingdom.

In the face of all this, it is one of the major surprises of getting around the map to discover how many ministers have

178

married the right women, chosen in extreme youth but whittled away by time and shock into very useful saints and ladies; with the drum of the Eternal regulating their footsteps, with the dream of harvest deep in their souls and the zeal of rescue foremost in their loneliness.

For the minister's wife as I see her is lonely—not so much so if she is of the extrovert type who likes everybody with equal enjoyment, easily sharing all the thoughts which lie on the top of her mind; but indeed lonely if she is of the quieter introvert type, silently bearing the whole parish in her heart. Of what is she thinking at any given moment? You cannot tell! For she gives no inkling. But if across the years you add this scattered sentence to that scattered sentence, and this detached gesture to that detached gesture, you can build up patiently the little sream of consciousness which courses constantly through her mind in church. For example, watching the congregation as her husband preaches: Oh, why doesn't he get a fresher illustration for that point in his sermon? Such as? Well, it evades her at the moment; but mentally she makes a note to find some apt tidbit to lay on his desk casually; not tomorrow, for it may be a blue Monday, but surely Tuesday morning would be an auspicious moment. Yes, indeed, watch any minister's wife on various occasions diving surreptitiously into her purse for a scrap of paper to jot down hastily a telling simile, a glowing story to enliven her husband's barrel. It is the farmer's wife at work, collecting seeds for a richer harvest.

Dip a little deeper into her stream of consciousness; watch her eyes roving over the congregation, naming over the local saints, present and absent, almost as a nun tells her beads. Good gracious, Mr. A missing again! What on earth can this mean? Not illness, for she saw him on the street only yesterday in the pink of perfection. Indifference, then? Neglect? Hurt feelings? *"O dear God, please don't let Mr. A get immersed again in worldly affairs!"* It's the lighthouse keeper's wife, bent on the exciting rescue of Mr. A, finally setting him up on some prominent rock, suggesting his name as chairman of this or that, pushing Mrs. A forward, and all the little A's as well, giving them parts in pageants and solos in cantatas, concerned over each and every member of the flock, wherever storms are brewing. No, all this can never be told, for she does it unconsciously; but watch the eyes of the minister's wife going quietly from pew to pew with lovely and lively concern, noticing who is bored, who is eager, who is troubled. From A to Z they are all hers, and of a Sabbath morning she is recording their life and state of preservation.

You never gauge the minister's wife aright until you remember this four-ring circus of her activities: *aquarium, farm, lighthouse, army;* for it is in the midst of constant publicity, planting, phosphorescence, and parading that she lives out her days, sublimating her selfish love of privacy, sowing all sorts of seeds in all sorts of sinners, shining serenely up above the shipwrecks of the saints, signaling to shoddy soldiers. It's a tall order. Yet I see her any day accomplishing it with dignity and skill, and bringing up children besides!

To be brought up in a fishbowl is a terrible business. A whole congregation forever ringing the doorbell or phoning messages which must be remembered verbatim. A whole congregation commenting on the cold in your nose or the state of your shoes. A whole congregation expecting you not to wriggle in church and to remember all the golden texts clear back to the year 1. Also the tongue-tied discipline of never repeating what has been said at the parsonage dinner table, and the higher discipline of letting a tenth of the family income go back into the church treasury instead of turning it into skates, bicycles, neckties, sweaters. Somehow the minister's wife has managed to pack such meaning behind the aquarium, farm, and lighthouse aspects of clerical life that her children can accept even the purse-string restraints; and evidently her interpretation has been genuine, for ministers' sons are not as black as they are painted—not, judging from the prowess of parsonage children, conspicuously in the top ranks of sociological, philanthropic, literary, and scientific enterprises, not to mention the preachers who come out of the parsonage. Life on a shoestring has been convincing enough to make children copy their parents, and this is tribute indeed to the minister's wife as I see her.

Surely the salary needs a paragraph or two all to itself. For the membership, having licked it into weekly duplex envelopes, often finds a secret fascination in watching it at work the following month, buying groceries, blooming into bonnets, or dashing down the street in the minister's old car. The smaller the church and the poorer the congregation, the more conscious they are of parsonage expenditures; and the more the minister's wife hesitates over her purchases, especially if it be new clothes when old ones really might last out another season. One such lady with a tendency toward sainthood always had a temporary setback when the choir sang its favorite anthem, "Nothing Changes Here"; for her perennial plain gray suit grew plainer and grayer as the years went by.

If the average income of the flock is less than the minister receives, then nobody wants to hear the minister or his wife use that bitter sentence, "We can't afford to," when their minister apparently can afford far more than they can. Apparently; but not actually. For on the clergyman's side is a constant series of demands which the congregation rarely considers—such as the need to read widely, keeping abreast of new books in every possible field because here are his meat and drink, with all those lively quotations his wife is forever seeking. Then there is the matter of college for the children, and post-graduate studies as well, which the average parishioner does not dream of including in his similar limited budget.

Nobody ever lists the minister's wife among America's ten leading financiers; yet that is where she definitely belongs. For who else can stretch a dollar quite so far? Foremost in her stream of consciousness floats the pastoral motto: "We can do without it." It is thus that ladies turn into saints, incidentally: one less potato + one less chop + one less bonnet + one less hairnet + one less pair of shoes has managed to put a child through many a next semester. Even more drastic parings-down have gone into another necessity which the everyday member of the flock does not suspect is so essential, namely, the vacation. To get far, far away from even the most devoted parishioners, to drop their combined sins and sorrows at the edge of some forest primeval, to become gloriously a released soul—this is ministerial life, liberty, and the pursuit of happiness. But four weeks away from home cost real money, and eight weeks can empty a purse. For what the bookstore, the college, and the summer outing have not consumed, the duplex envelope has eaten up beforehand. The tithe! It is an innocent word which half the congregation leaves contentedly enough to the Jews; but the minister's family have placed it first on their budget, and it is from daily wrestlings with finances that the minister's wife sometimes arrives at church a little breathless.

Aside from all this private life in her fishbowl, into which the membership sees as in a glass darkly, there is all her public life which he who runs may read. For the minister's wife as I see her falls into one of two categories: either she belongs to her husband in toto, on the theory that he receives the salary, so that, like any other wife, she is the keeper of his home, the mother of his children, and can come to church with gloves on, like any other woman; or she belongs to the flock in toto, on the theory that she and her husband are partners in this highly exacting farm-lighthouse-army enterprise, so that she must take off her gloves and go to work with might and main.

There are all sorts of things you can say and think and approve of in both attitudes, but the best sidelight I ever heard a minister's wife throw on her life concerned her gradual shift in emphasis. She said that at first she dreamed of a tombstone, put up by the membership on some dim distant day, chiseled to read:

SHE DID THE WORK OF TEN WOMEN

But with the passage of years, she began altering the desired wording until it might say:

SHE DID THE WORK OF ONE WOMAN WELL
AND SET THE OTHER NINE TO WORKING

For this is, of course, the wholesome and the truly educational thing to do, since next year any minister may be called to Oshkosh. Why leave all the work at Podunk totally crippled because the minister's wife has stepped out from under? To have trained and trusted an understudy is a gracious and enduring monument; and it is no bromide to use the oft-quoted phrasing that years later the people "will rise up and call her blessed."

And now for the lovely fun of sharing with you the secret things the minister's wife does not like at all about church life. She does not like having no intimates. We are all born needing trusted favorites, but the minister's wife as I see her rarely is willing to create church jealousies by choosing one such conspicuous friend to whom she unburdens her mind. She dislikes all this caution. She dislikes knowing that certain persons boast about her friendship behind her back. She finds something subtly annoying in the little tinge of pride which flicks across the face of such a person when she calls her by her first name. "Good gracious, she's all set up over knowing me!" she groans. This is not friendship but a taste of "privilege," and she dislikes it.

She does not like anything which puts her up on a pedestal, since being a statue is tedious business—the pose wearies; the noblest smile begins to dangle from the cheekbones; the softest answer turns a little artificial. No, she does not like being considered "very, very good." She remembers the little curl in the middle of her forehead, and wonders what would happen if she were very, very horrid. But she never is. And she dislikes this too, sometimes!

Above all, she does not like to open the door of a room where a meeting has begun, to walk innocently toward a seat, and then to have these dire words fall on her ears: "Oh, here is our minister's wife! Mrs. Smith, would you lead us in prayer?" Instant relief in the voice of the chairman. Instant consternation in the voice of the minister's wife. You can hear her waver uncertainly as she tries to push a dozen details out of her mind: Mrs. B's rheumatism, Mr. C's change of address, Miss D's appointment, not to mention the carrots left cooking on the parsonage stove, wasting gas and vitamins. In lovely, meek despair she begins: "O Lord . . . ." and He alone seems to realize that this is really a comment rather than a prayer! For the minister's wife knows that worship is a precious, rare experience; and just when she least wants to fumble, she can't for the life of her remember the topic of the meeting. Is it home or foreign missions? Or a purely local matter? So she encompasses the globe, covering land and sea; and the Lord in His deep understanding probably finds it an adequate uplifting of this little handful of His flock. But she knows, and the audience guesses, that she hadn't an idea what to say next.

Neither does she like being the final authority in every crisis! Or, if she does like it, she realizes that the lady in her is triumphing over the saint, loving power and glory beyond what is expedient. She does not like being made chairman of committees when no one else is willing to bear the brunt of the work involved, but here is where the saint triumphs over the lady. "It's your fatal pride which is touched, my good woman! You hate being the last choice instead of the first." But because she cares for the work more than for herself, she takes on each larger burden; and many a day her halo is actually visible, even to the naked eye.

The halo disappears considerably when she is asked inquisitive questions about her husband. And as for being told how to bring up her children! Neither does she like hearing gossip about one member of the church from another member. These are by no means generalizations so wide that they have no flesh and blood; look at your own minister's wife carefully some day and you can see that they all are true.

Amusingly enough, she does not always like having her husband forever at home, "under foot," as it were. Where other housewives are free to scrub and scour by day, with the radio going full tilt to while away the hours, she always has this tense and temperamental preacher on hand, forever in the midst of finishing one sermon only to begin another—which

185

means tiptoeing gently over his head, hushing the children, subduing the dog, leaping to the telephone, creating around him the "silence of heaven for the space of half an hour" so that he can "see the seven angels . . . . and God."

And having a man at home for every meal is not the easiest thing in the world. A whole chapter could be devoted to parsonage meals. Needless to say, they must cost next to nothing, and yet they must be wholesome and nourishing for a man whose job is so exacting. Yet such meals must take a minimum of preparation, when morning meetings last far over the noon hour; and, in some magical way, the food must stay hot until the last parishioner has let the minister come home. Moreover, all clerical food must be somewhat elastic, so that it can stretch if company comes. And to avoid comments, it must never look either too rich or too stingy. Martha must be the favorite Bible character of many a minister's wife, pestered with much serving. Yet all the time it is the Mary side of her nature which she truly values the most.

It would be unfair to leave out the things the minister's wife enjoys especially. Foremost is the delight of seeing young people grow up and become pillars, to see an ideal at work in their lives after years of planting. No farmer's wife ever looks at a golden harvest with half the joy of a minister's wife when a new Christian home embodies her dream. There is no pleasure equal to the honest devotion of a congregation—the sincere attention paid to suggestions, the eager acknowledgment of leadership, the genuine heartbreak when the call to another parish is accepted. These are the precious things which enrich the lives of every minister's family, along with the mutual tenderness at times of sickness, the mutual concern at times of sorrows.

When the minister's wife is completely frank with herself—more saint than lady!—she knows how perilously sweet it is to be a little more skilled than anyone else, because of so many varied experiences; to be a little more consulted than anyone else, because of position; to be able to get one's own way a little more easily than anyone else. Yes, this is dangerously dear; how dear one knows only when it has suddenly slipped away into the lost-and-found department of life. Her husband has become now General Secretary of this or that in the denomination, let us say; traveling endlessly, no longer underfoot, no longer available to hammer a nail or share the latest news. And there is no parishioner to telephone sympathetically about her sore throat, etc. She begins to think back with surprise at the snug little dignity of living in a fishbowl, forever watched, forever stretched upward to be her best, forever needed and called on. . . . . Why, the half has never been told!

But only the minister's widow has the total loss; for she sees another woman doing either better or worse in her very shoes, and she must still discipline her public behavior and her private pain. For now there is no one she can share things with, she who never could share anything except with the farmer as he fed his flock and with the lighthouse keeper as he rescued those in danger. Yes, those were indeed the days! Rich and full and vivid. Her very furniture becomes reminiscent.

"This was the chair from Bill's father's attic; he thought it would be plenty good enough to begin with. And now it is plenty good enough to end with! I still remember the day one of my Sunday school girls sat in that chair telling me that my way of living had changed her entire philosophy of life. So off she went to China; and now she's principal of that important school, helping to swing a whole province into Christianity.

Who would have thought a foolish creature such as I could ever work such a miracle, when just a short while before I had been hankering for silly new bonnets! Then, quite suddenly, to discover how immensely more exciting to transpose my entire head to younger shoulders—dreams and all! Oh, those were the days!"

Yes, you can almost always tell a saint from a lady. Not so much on account of the halo of the one as on account of the hat of the other. For the lady's always has considerably more style. But the saint goes around creating new fashions! Everywhere on earth you will find her followers: big churches, little churches. The people will say: "Yes, Dr. So-and-So was a remarkable preacher—a regular prima donna; he just gave himself to it. But Mrs. So-and-So always remembered my name!"

Of course she did.

For down in her heart the minister's wife is nothing but a shepherdess. This business about aquarium, army, and lighthouse is all rhetoric. But being a shepherdess is endearing and rewarding; she does it because it comes natural, and she loves it.

WHO WROTE THIS BOOK?

THE EDITOR

GOLDA ELAM BADER is the wife of Dr. Jesse M. Bader, executive secretary of the Department of Evangelism of the Federal Council of the Churches of Christ in America. She was educated at Drake University, the Sorbonne, and the University of Mexico, and has traveled around the world and spent much time in various nations. She is an ordained minister and has served in two churches as associate pastor. She has been chairman of the Ministers' Wives' Association of New York City and of the Women's Division of the National Conference of Christians and Jews. She lives in New York City.

I. PORTRAIT OF A MINISTER'S WIFE

BESS WHITE COCHRAN married, not a minister, but a lawyer, Louis Cochran. Her portrait is of her mother, Frances Atkins White, who did marry a minister, Dr. Walter M. White, for many years pastor of Linden Avenue Christian Church, Memphis, Tennessee. Mrs. Cochran was educated at Transylvania College and the University of Michigan, and traveled and studied two summers in Europe. She has been a newspaper reporter, editor of *World Call,* and publicity director for the National Benevolent Association. Her home is in Santa Monica, California.

II. HER CHURCH

PRISCILLA WAHL STAMM, wife of Bishop John S. Stamm, has had varied experience as a minister's wife during her husband's career as pastor, professor of theology, president of a seminary, and now senior bishop of the Evangelical Church. She is chairman of the Woman's Department of the Board of Missions of the Evangelical Church, and in interdenominational work has been vice-president of the Woman's Department of the Pennsylvania Council of Churches, a member of the Woman's Committee of the Foreign Missions Conference, and a member of the Executive Committee of the Council of Women for Home Missions. She lives in Harrisburg, Pennsylvania.

III. HER PRIVILEGES

GRACE TILTON SHULLENBERGER is the wife of Dr. William A. Shullenberger, pastor of Central Christian Church, Indianapolis, Indiana. She was educated at the Sherwood School of Music in Chicago and the College of Fine Arts of Drake University. With her husband she was a fraternal delegate to the British Churches of Christ and to the World Convention of the Disciples of Christ. She has been president of the National Council of Ministers' Wives, and a member of the board of the Council of Church Women, of the Board of Trustees of the United Christian Missionary Society, and of the P.E.O. Sisterhood. She has three sons.

WHO WROTE THIS BOOK?

IV. HER OPPORTUNITIES

Georgiana Sibley Glenn is the wife of the Rev. C. Leslie Glenn, rector of St. John's Episcopal Church, Washington, D. C. The mother of three young children, she finds time to be superintendent of her church school; national vice-president of the Girl Scouts; chairman of the Speakers' Bureau of the Washington Civilian Volunteer Defense Bureau; chairman of the Senior Northfield Conference; board member for St. John's Orphanage, the House of Mercy, and the Washington Council of Church Women; and a member of the Junior League.

V. HER WIDER OUTLOOK

Winifred Mead Clinchy is the wife of Dr. Everett Ross Clinchy, Presbyterian minister and director of the National Conference of Christians and Jews; and is the daughter of Methodist Bishop and Mrs. Charles L. Mead. She is a graduate of the University of Denver and a former president of the Y. W. C. A. of Morris County, New Jersey. She lives in Pottersville, New Jersey, and has a son and two daughters.

VI. HER SPIRITUAL LIFE

Lillian Diebold Poling is the wife of Dr. Daniel A. Poling, pastor of the Baptist Temple of Philadelphia, Pennsylvania, and president of the International Society of Christian Endeavor. After majoring in home economics at Ohio State University, she was a teacher before marriage. She founded the Little Nell House, a demonstration "good neighbor" house; the Monday Fellowship of Prayer; the Philadelphia Religion in Life Group; and has been educational chairman of the Woman's Division War Camp Community Service, and president of the Council of Women for Home Missions. She is the mother of eight children.

VII. HER HOME

Ruth Stafford Peale is the wife of Dr. Norman Vincent Peale, pastor of the Marble Collegiate Reformed Church of New York City. After graduation from Syracuse University, she was a high school teacher until her marriage to Dr. Peale, at that time pastor of the University Methodist Church in Syracuse. Mrs. Peale is president of the Women's Board of Domestic Missions of the Reformed Church, vice-president of the Home Missions Council of North America, and a member of the Executive Committee of the Federal Council of the Churches of Christ in America, and of the United Council of Church Women. Her own home is complete with three children.

VIII. HER CHILDREN

Nellie Snoke Brewbaker is the wife of Dr. Charles W. Brewbaker, pastor of the Fairview United Brethren Church of Dayton, Ohio. She is a graduate of the State Teachers' College of Shippensburg, Pennsylvania, and was a teacher before marriage. Her two daughters have testified to their satisfaction with being children of the parsonage by themselves marrying ministers: Dr. John Ruskin Howe, president of Otterbein College, and the Rev. Robert Copeland, pastor of the historic United Brethren Church at Germantown, Ohio.

IX. HER FRIENDS

MARY HANSFORD BROWN is the wife of Dr. Frank Chilton Brown, pastor of the First Presbyterian Church of Dallas, Texas, since 1936, and formerly pastor of the Bream Memorial Presbyterian Church, Charleston, West Virginia, for many years. She is a native West Virginian and has studied at Columbia University, a music school in Chicago, and a Trinity term at Oxford University. She has traveled extensively in Europe and the Holy Land.

X. HER APPEARANCE

LILIE BENBOW SCHERER is the wife of Dr. Paul Scherer, pastor of the Holy Trinity Lutheran Church of New York City. Her paternal grandfather was called from Wales to lead the Welsh singers of Ohio; and when she was born in Reading, Pennsylvania, her father was organist of Holy Trinity Church, where her maternal grandfather was for thirty years the minister. She is a graduate of Dana Hall, Wellesley, Massachusetts, and of the New York State Normal School, where she specialized in kindergarten work. She has been active in the Y. W. C. A., directing activities of high school girls and industrial workers. She has two daughters.

XI. HER AVOCATION

JEAN BEAVEN ABERNETHY is the wife of Dr. Bradford S. Abernethy, secretary of the Commission to Study the Bases of a Just and Durable Peace of the Federal Council of the Churches of Christ in America, and former pastor of the First Baptist Church, Columbia, Missouri; and is the daughter of President Albert W. Beaven of Colgate-Rochester Divinity School. She is a Phi Beta Kappa graduate of Mount Holyoke, and studied with her husband in Edinburgh and Oxford. She now writes, lectures, and teaches part time in a junior college. She lives in White Plains, New York, and has two small children.

XII. HER SPECIAL INTERESTS

MAE TALMAGE PRUDEN is the wife of Dr. Edward Hughes Pruden, pastor of the First Baptist Church of Washington, D. C. She is a graduate in piano of the Cincinnati Conservatory of Music and has appeared as soloist with several symphony orchestras. With her husband she spent a year in China, both teaching in the University of Shanghai. She has two children.

XIII. HER HOBBIES

MADELEINE SWEENY MILLER is the wife of Dr. J. Lane Miller, pastor of the Hanson Place Central Methodist Church in Brooklyn, New York. She is a

Phi Beta Kappa graduate of Vassar College. With her husband she has traveled much, studying places, buildings, and works of art connected with the growth of Christianity. Her journeys, as well as her other "hobbies," she has written about in many articles and a number of books, among which are *Footprints in Palestine, New Testament Women and Problems of Today, Church Pageantry, My Hobby of the Cross,* and, with her husband, *Cruising the Mediterranean.*

XIV. HER VACATIONS

HELEN MITCHELL GIBSON is the wife of Dr. Robert W. Gibson, pastor of the historic Third United Presbyterian Church of Pittsburgh, Pennsylvania. She is a native of Ohio and a graduate of Muskingum College, and taught in a high school before her marriage. She has a daughter and a son.

XV. FROM A COUNTRY PARSONAGE WINDOW

MARY HEALD WILLIAMSON is the wife of the Rev. Ralph L. Williamson, rural secretary of the New York State Council of Churches and field secretary of the Rural Institute. She is a graduate of Iowa State College and taught social science before her marriage. Along with her husband, she has been most active in rural work, lecturing on the rural church and home, leading conferences of rural ministers' wives, and serving as rural chairman of the New York State Council of Church Women. She is assistant editor of the *New York Christian Rural Fellowship Bulletin,* contributes to many farm and religious periodicals, and has written two books. She lives in Trumansburg, New York, and has three sons.

XVI. I MARRIED A RABBI

RUTH WOLF LEVI is the wife of Dr. Harry Levi, rabbi of Temple Israel, Boston, Massachusetts, since 1911. She was educated at Mount de Chantal Academy, Wheeling, West Virginia, and is a graduate of the Cincinnati College of Music. She is active in various women's groups in the Boston area. She has two sons.

XVII. SAINTS AND LADIES AND MINISTERS' WIVES

MARGARET T. APPLEGARTH is not a minister's wife but has had many opportunities to observe the species in her contacts as a lecturer with the National Christian Mission and before other church groups, women's clubs, parent-teacher associations, and story-tellers' leagues; as a member of various national interdenominational boards; and as chairman of the American Committee of the World Day of Prayer, which plans the universal programs and observances in fifty-one countries of the world. She edits a monthly magazine in Braille for blind boys and girls, and is author of more than thirty books, of which the latest is *Bound in the Bundle of Life.*